A Yankee Jazz Singer in Cuzco

Other works by John P. Calu

Touchy, Feely Crap   2002, iUniverse, Inc.

With Co-Author David A. Hart

The Treasure of Tucker's Island	2003, iUniverse, Inc.
Mystery of the Jersey Devil	2005, iUniverse, Inc.
Secret of the Painted Rock	2006, iUniverse, Inc.
The Lost Mission of Captain Carranza	2007, iUniverse, Inc
Riddle in the Sand	2009, iUniverse, Inc
Trenton, a Novel	2010 Plexus Publishing, Inc
Spirits of Cedar Bridge	2012, iUniverse, Inc

For more information, please visit:

www.ch-artworks.com

www.trentonthenovel.com

A Yankee Jazz Singer in Cuzco

John P. Calu

iUniverse LLC
Bloomington

A YANKEE JAZZ SINGER IN CUZCO

iUniverse books may be ordered through booksellers or by contacting:

iUniverse
1663 Liberty Drive
Bloomington, IN 47403
www.iuniverse.com
1-800-Authors (1-800-288-4677)

Because of the dynamic nature of the Internet, any web addresses or links contained in this book may have changed since publication and may no longer be valid.

The views expressed in this work are solely those of the author and do not necessarily reflect the views of the publisher, and the publisher hereby disclaims any responsibility for them.

Any people depicted in stock imagery provided by Thinkstock are models, and such images are being used for illustrative purposes only. Certain stock imagery © Thinkstock.

ISBN: 978-1-4917-1070-8 (sc)
ISBN: 978-1-4917-1071-5 (e)

Printed in the United States of America.

iUniverse rev. date: 10/17/2013

For Vanessa
Go Out & Find Your Passion, Honey
Herein Lies Mine

Acknowledgments

First and Foremost, my unending gratitude goes to Zully & Vanessa Calu for their love, laughter and devotion to all that is good in this world. Many thanks to Dave Hart for sharing a vision and the work ethic needed to get there. Thanks also to Michelle Hart for following in her father's footsteps and writing so brilliantly that she inspires us both. I don't know what I'd do without Rich Klupp, Daniel McAuliffe & Paul Garvin, my bonfire brethren who know how to share life's generous bounty. To Randy, Chic, Marcelo, Andres & Luis—the distance is gone in an instant and the connections remain true. To Bob Stives, Tim Bullock, Jack Warwick & John Swatkoski—your friendship is a source of strength, filled with wonderful memories. To John Bryans, Mike Pippin, Linda Stanton, Rob Colding, Nancy Ellor, Dick Gratton, Chris Stopero, Jim Carlucci, Janie Hermann, Krystal Knapp & Leila Nogueira your encouragement and support have meant more to me than I could ever express. To Bob Lewis, thank you for helping me find my voice.

Table of Contents

The Art of Conversation...1

Hairless Tongue 3

My Friend the Shaman 5

I Often Dream in Spanish 7

Clothes Horse...9

A Reasonable Life 11

Sunday Dinner...13

Candy Hearts & Flowers 15

Bon Vivant...17

A World Away 19

In Memory of ATC...21

Grace 23

A Yankee Jazz Singer in Cuzco.......................................25

Tuesday Night Jazz..27

Reunion 29

The Heart of the Matter 31

R.I.P. ETTA 33

Momentarily Vegetarian 35

The Third Act 37

Accounting versus Reckoning 39

"Brother, can you spare a dime?" 41

All in 43

The Peacemakers...45

The Grand Bazaar 47

Hurricane Season 49

The Next Frontier...51

SongFactory..53

Archetypes 55

Only in America...57

Univision 59

To Have & Have Not 61

Joseph Campbell said to Jump! 63

Bonfire 65

First, Do No Harm 67

Barnyard Battles 69

A Summer Camp in Maine 71

Here's To Tomorrow 73

Feliz Cinco 75

Concert for the Moons 77

The Seventies 79

Made In Bangalore? 81

Spanish Guitar 83

Gato Negro 85

All Kinds of Barbecue 87

DNA 89

Backstage 91

The Sounds of Silence 93

Femme Phrenale 95

BYOB 97

SongMaker 99

Home is where the art is 101

Abundant Lives 103

The Art of Conversation

There's nothing wrong with small talk. In fact, sometimes I prefer it. When you're in a crowd of people or meeting someone for the first time, it's tough to discuss the most intimate details of your life or challenge someone to define a philosophy that guides their every move.

Small talk takes on different contexts in different settings. In a suburban house party, it could be lawn care, property taxes and pre-packaged hors d'oeuvres. In a hip mid town soiree it could be Magritte, method acting in Swiss minimalist cinema and baked brie. On a Texas ranch, it could be pork futures, raising cattle, barbecue recipes and the price of gold. At an upscale old money country club it could be finding good help, hedging one's bets and thriving on the back nine.

You can either use small talk to get to know more about someone or to avoid talking about more important subjects. That's your call and I respect it either way. I may not stick around very long if the conversation remains that limited, but I can play a patient enough social game to time my exit without offending anyone. I think of conversation as an artform and not everyone likes the same canvas, concerto or banquet fare.

When you get past the civilities, people tend to go into the biographies and that's the step I like skipping the most. I've been to Spain. You've been to Paris. I went to grammar school. You went to Choate. I've got a Hyundai. You've got a pension fund. I sell shingles. You steal pearls. You like boys and I like girls. No offense, but I don't really care much about where I've been let alone where you've been. I'm far more interested in where we're at today and where we want to be tomorrow. We can reminisce about the way we spent our roaring twenties, the mountains we climbed in our thirties and forties and the things we conquered along the way. But doesn't it make sense to accept that those adventures have already informed us and use the time we have today to make new and exciting discoveries?

There are two kinds of conversation I really enjoy the most. One is when I get the opportunity to talk with someone who has a passion for something. It doesn't even matter what that passion is for—as long as they're willing to share it. I've listened with great joy to a man describe a fishing trip in the great lakes and I probably wouldn't be caught dead there no matter what the lure. I was thrilled to hear a painter friend detail the importance of arches in both energy and design and I haven't got enough skill to draw a straight line. The other kind of conversation I enjoy is when two or more participants are willing to shed themselves entirely for the benefit of wherever the conversation might take them. It's hard to do because it's hard to get out of our own way let alone deny our own stubborn point of view in favor of whatever consensus develops organically. When we let a conversation grow from abstract concepts and share perspectives based upon both individual and universal experiences, it can get pretty heady and offer lots of fun and tender insights into the human condition. Nice talking with you.

Hairless Tongue

It is incredibly easy to stereotype, isn't it? As I passed a service station this morning on my way to drop my daughter off at school, she mentioned that a kid from her high school had gotten a part time job there, "and he's white," she added with some surprise, explaining that she thought only people from India or Pakistan ever got hired there. A few weeks ago she went to a junior prom in another part of the state and noticed that everybody there was "white" compared to our multi-racial community.

People may find this hard to believe but I was one of those "eyetalian" kids who grew up in a white working class neighborhood and even though my mom was English and Irish with a smidgeon of Lenape Indian blood, having an "eyetalian" father ensured that we were regarded much like the Hispanics in those same neighborhoods are today. We were nice people as long as we didn't throw too many ethnic house parties and took good care of our lawn. I guess my Peruvian wife and I along with our mixed race daughter could still be considered a novelty in some neighborhoods, but thankfully we live in a very diverse community where an economic democracy is hard at work. In other words, if you've got the money to live here we don't care what race, color, creed or sexual identity you represent. We all know there are both upscale and low rent districts that have a decidedly different outlook on life and I wouldn't want to live in either of those worlds.

I once naively asked a group of young basketball players from the Ivory Coast if everyone in their country was "black." You should have heard the white folks around me gasp. The black guys laughed out loud at my ignorance and my lack of tact. In Spanish, they say "el no tiene pelos en la lengua" which translates into "he's got no hairs on his tongue." Creates an unpleasant image I know, but it actually means "he'll say whatever the hell he's thinking, regardless of who might hear him."

If you could have locked my dad in a room with a Swiss gardener, a Japanese pastry chef, a Mexican scientist and an African economist, he would have found a common denominator and become their beloved leader within a couple hours. Just like most men growing up how and where he did, he had deeply engrained stereotypes and prejudices, but he never let that get in the way of developing a bond with a decent individual no matter what their race, religion or socio-political affiliation. I hope I'm half the man he was in that regard.

I knew a bartender in California years ago, who was a different type of sexual predator. He was an American guy married to a lovely British woman, but he prided himself on having had sex with men and women of every nationality on earth. He actually hit on me trying to score a Native American man, but luckily lost interest when he found out I was half "eyetalian." Like I said, "no hairs on my tongue," thank heaven!

My Friend the Shaman

Randy comes to town once or twice a year for pinelands explorations led by acclaimed tracker, Tom Brown. His most recent visit was a few weeks ago. He flew in on Alaska Airlines from Seattle by way of Spokane and I picked him up at Newark Airport, around five in the evening. He'd had a long day, but you'd never know it from the way he greeted me or the way our visit unfolded over the next eighteen hours.

We started our conversation over twenty-five years ago on the screened in back porch of a ranch house in Lake Grove, Connecticut where Randy was setting up a summer camp to serve the needs of mildly autistic children and young adults. He hired me to help the young, mostly European counselors develop a creative writing, music and drama program based upon something called SongFactory which I had left behind in California the year before. He had heard about it at Jane Fonda's ranch in Santa Barbara and decided to track me down in New Jersey. At the time, I was an unsuccessful music producer singing jazz to keep my muse amused and drinking more than my fair share to numb the pain of recent commercial failures. I didn't know what he saw in me or why he insisted that I give it a try, but I will never be able to thank him enough.

The camp was a modest success and we both moved on with our lives, the better for having shared the experience. We've stayed in touch pretty regularly ever since. I went on a South American sojourn, to write the great American novel (which I still haven't published) and Randy went on to become an educator and a psychologist. He also went and got himself adopted by the Lakota Sioux and trained as a Shaman. I just love saying, "my friend the Shaman" to see how people will react. It would be more appropriate however to say my brother, the Shaman because we are far closer than the term friend alone would indicate.

Randy and I have spent a thousand hours together in deep philosophical discussions and barely scraped the surface. We have a connection that has lasted through gain and loss, time and tide, strengthening with each new visit based upon something we both learned a long time ago and continue to practice every time we meet again.

The best thing you can ever give anyone is to be present when you are with them. That's worth repeating. The best thing you can ever give anyone is to be present when you are with them.

I Often Dream in Spanish . . .

The air was so warm and dry on a summer night in Seville that men walked behind their wives just to catch the breeze afforded by the movement of their pleated skirts, not to mention the inspiring view. The fans used by flamenco dancers found their way into every woman's purse and nothing quenched their thirst as sweetly as the rich red sangria flowing from a generous, if a little lecherous, bartender who nonetheless introduced me to the woman sitting next to me.

She took my hand in front of a cathedral. There was one on every corner and I don't recall the patron saint of this one in particular. It might have been Erasmus as in Erasmus be dragging since we'd walked a few hundred blocks that night to find a highly touted hideaway called Montenegro. The floor show was professional enough, but couldn't rival the smoldering glances exchanged by members of the audience tingling with the heat of the night itself.

You had the feeling if a gaze had lingered a moment too long, it would have been enough to light a tinderbox of sensual abandon or at least provoke a fight defending the honor of whoever you had flirted with so carelessly. Husbands held their wives hands in plain view of the men around them offering a pretense of possession. Women bared as much of their legs as they could and stared at each other fiercely through laughing eyes, challenging one another to capture the attention of the most virile male among them. The rhythm of the guitars threatened the beating of feint hearts as the evening sizzled out of control. Dancers stirred the saucy air and fanned the flames of every man and woman's desire.

Couples coupled and recoupled, some along the riverbank and others in the park. We made our way back to my hotel groping in the dark. That night a thousand ceiling fans overheard our passion play and do not disturb signs were proudly on display.

In the morning after coffee on my balcony, we kissed goodbye. She did not care to know my name and refused my request for her number. I suggested we return to where we'd met and she smiled at my poor romantic gesture. "They're only open on Tuesdays and I'm going somewhere else tonight," she replied in a deep sultry voice. I asked if I could go there with her and she told me I would have to find her first then ran away.

Many years later I heard high heels clicking behind me on the street one night and turned around certain for some reason it was her. An old flamenco dancer smiled at me lasciviously and there was a strangely familiar twinkle in her eye. "They're only open on Tuesdays then we dance at Montenegro," she smiled and added "I'm glad you finally found me."

Clothes Horse

I'm wearing a shirt my wife's best friend likes. She complimented me on it once and that's not something she normally does. It's sort of a royal blue, Pima cotton button down made in Peru. It's soft, luxurious, yet masculine and contrasts wonderfully with a black sport coat and my salt and pepper hair. I've worn it to book signings with a hope of looking hip.

I think men's fashion began for me at an early age. My father was a dapper son of a gun who loved to sport a nice blue blazer, white shirt with gray slacks, cordovan brogues and a regimental striped tie. We considered this an Ivy League look and strolled to church in Mercerville as if we were expected later somewhere off of Nassau Street in Princeton. In fact, we once bought underwear and socks at Bamberger's on Harrison Street and felt like we had roots in the community.

Luckily my mom and dad were bargain hunters which enabled me to become the clothes horse I am today. We shopped in many of the finer establishments and specialty shops of the day, but always found our way to the clearance racks and discount bins intent on finding something others had failed to recognize the value in. Back in those days, you had to tell quality by the fabric and construction of the garment itself since designer's names and labels hadn't reached the point of all pervasive and we couldn't tell a Givenchy from a St. Laurent if our lives depended on it. The game has changed considerably today.

Okay, I'll admit it. I'm label conscious. I don't have a problem if you're not, but I get off on finding bargains that fit me well made by people who take my taste seriously enough to produce a quality product that appeals to me. I don't have to have this year's hot item until next year when I can afford it and I probably couldn't tell you what's hot this year anyway. I don't follow it that closely and I still have a penchant for those Ivy League roots I purchased long ago.

After my mom passed away, my father lived with my wife and me in Miami for a couple years. He taught my wife how to speak Jersey and how to shop for clothes. The former still gets more laughs than you can ever imagine and the latter has saved me a fortune over the years. My wife has graciously passed those skills on to our fashionable teenage daughter as well.

When I was a teenager, my uncle from Rhode Island gave me a Vicuña coat. Even though it was handed down to him by a Mafia don with more money than he knew what to do with, what I marveled at most was how the label said it came from the mountains of Peru. Who knew I would get to see where it came from someday and pick up a shirt to go with it at a price you wouldn't believe.

A Reasonable Life

Angst and appreciation both come in all shapes and sizes. Taking a cue from Native American philosophy we can all rest assured that the one we feed will be the one that grows.

There are people among us who struggle daily with life limiting conditions and life threatening illnesses. Many have lost parents. Some have lost spouses and others have even lost children. Some have lost their jobs or they battle with addictions. Others have simply lost their way. Can we pause a moment for all of them and pray?

Spend some time in silence on behalf of those for whom this life is far too loud. Gaze lovingly into the sunrise for those among us who cannot see. Listen to soft music for those who cannot hear. Dance for those still longing to be free. Drink deep the bounty you are blessed to receive and pray you never lose compassion for those who grieve.

This is not an easy journey between birth and whatever lies beyond. First we must awaken to a body that needs nurturing and protection. It comes without instructions and in some sad cases without decent role models to guide us. We are only briefly allowed to enjoy an imagination before we are thrust into a system designed to make that harder with each passing year.

As our bodies mature, our spirits are challenged. We are tempted by our natural desires and driven to achieve the impossible. We explore, expand, create and command. We divine, devise, design and construct. We fuel, fit, facilitate, imitate and initiate. We charge headlong with sheer determination and accomplish miracles without consideration of the ruins we leave in our wake. The world is ours to take. The world is ours to break.

At some point, life begins to teach us what we failed to take the time to learn. Through loss and longing we are tempered and shown what our efforts have earned. The younger we start to walk lightly, the more gentle the world becomes. We can still scale the heights and rest in green valleys beside rivers we don't have to outrun.

We wonder if a sage is born or becomes that way through age. Is wisdom not part weary, part wary, part sad and part glad for having passed this way before? Is joy not part reach, part peace, part pace and part embrace of those things which we need no more? At a certain point in time, a reasonable life finds its rhyme. And man at a certain state, begins to accept his fate. There are two wolves at your door. Give thanks, there are no more.

Sunday Dinner

She must have gotten up pretty early because the dining room table was already set with fresh flowers and a plate of cheese and meats next to a basket of hard crusted bread and a small glass pitcher of olive oil when we showed up at noon. The sauce and meatballs were on the stove and you could smell the garlic even before she opened the kitchen door. I watched her work the rolling pin over a sheet of flour dusted semolina. She cut it into squares and added a dollop of ricotta mixed with egg and curly parsley before folding them into neat little ravioli and gently pressing the edges closed.

The first course was usually a chicken broth with tiny little rice sized grains of macaroni I mistakenly thought was ditalini, but now I realize it was much smaller than that and more delicate. She sprinkled just a hint of pecorino Romano and added a touch of fresh ground black pepper to each bowl before placing two at a time on a small tray I would then take into the dining room. It was my first and best experience as a waiter, but I preferred to think of myself as the chef's assistant.

While my father and his brother swapped tales about the old country they had never been to and their two sisters sat gossiping in Italian and ignoring my mom as well as their other brother's wife even though she was Italian too, my brother and cousins must have been playing cards or something, because I was the only the kid in the kitchen with grand mom. The story goes that I teased her about being too fat to ride one horse and promised to get her two for the trip we'd be taking someday to California. I guess we were planning on visiting her cousins in the wine country. I don't know why else I would have wanted to go there at such a young age unless I intended to become a singing cowboy.

When the soup bowls were cleared, if memory serves me well, the pencil points with sauce and meatballs were served family style on a big platter. I don't think she made her own pencil points, but I'm sure she got them homemade from somewhere in the neighborhood. This was the one course she would actually sit down and eat with us, as soon as she had tossed together the fresh salad which would serve to separate this course from the next. When she and I had finished our meatballs, she nodded at me and I knew it was time to go get the salad and small plates with some more bread and butter this time for some reason I can't recall. While everybody else ate a little salad to help them digest the second course, she and I went back into the kitchen to prepare the next plate.

The chicken she had used to make the broth had been turned into cacciatore and she put a little of that over top a couple of hand made raviolis without covering them completely. She left room on each plate for the side dish I watched her take out of the oven. I had never seen her make it because she had to prep it the night before. She carefully cut the strings holding together artichokes stuffed with breadcrumbs and cheese and then drizzled a little olive oil on each before sending me out to hear the oohs and aahs. Her whole meal was incredible, but these were works of art, perfectly browned yet tender.

I don't remember coffee or tea. I was too young to notice or probably too full by that time, but I do remember sweet sticky fried dough with honey and powdered sugar, plus assorted cookies, nuts and orange sections ending the feast.

Over the years, I've tried to keep the tradition of a Sunday dinner alive, with modest success. I do love cooking and enjoy the company of friends and family around the table. If I could ever make you feel like you once had a seat at Concetta's table, you would understand why I have to do it. I never did get to take her to California, but I spent some time with her *paisanos* in wine country. They've always got a place at our table now too.

Candy Hearts & Flowers

It was tough approaching the prettiest girl in my third grade class. I watched her open my card and smile as she read the caption above the frog sitting on his lily . . . "I'd be HOPPY to share my PAD with you!" She handed me two candy hearts for my effort. One read "You're Sweet," and the other read "Buzz Off." I've been confused by Valentine's Day ever since.

In my late twenties, I managed to cook my first romantic dinner. I had the table set with candles and a nice white wine chilled to go with broiled seafood. The pasta was al dente and the salad was oh so fresh. Everything was perfect, except for the fact that my paramour du jour decided to extend an out of town visit for a threesome with her BFF and an old boyfriend from overseas.

Fast forward to sixteen years ago next week and I either did the least or most romantic thing you can ever imagine to honor the cupid or the stupid depending on your point of view. That was my first day on the job that still employs me. I've been through a few company buyouts and office relocations since then, but for the past sixteen heart shaped holidays I've been celebrating the anniversary of the day job that pays the bills.

My daughter was only a few months old then and I was lucky enough to find something steady that few people wanted to do and which has afforded us a clearly lavish lifestyle and kept the roof over our heads from leaking in the process.

Oh let's face it, I'm a romantic at heart. I want to be wined and dined and if no one else is going to do it for me, I'll do it for myself! I used to confuse a lot of women by cooking a decent meal and serving it with some flair. They thought it was my way of seducing them, but it was really just me being me. I don't have to worry about misleading anyone, anymore. These days I cook two or three meals a week and trust me, my wife isn't banging me daily in praise of my roast beef. I've got no complaints about our relations, but the way to her heart has never been that predictable.

So here comes the mushy part—turn the page if you can't handle it. I married a woman who amazes me. She's still a mystery after twenty-two years. She's stunning, intelligent, creative, passionate, artistic and ultimately kind. I have no idea what she sees in me, but the candy heart equivalent would clearly read "Be Mine."

Bon Vivant

As friends, family members and acquaintances get older we have a lot more discussions about quality of life issues such as when to pull the plug. I want to go on record here, in case anybody decides to question whether I really need that extra breath or not—as long as I'm still paying the bill for it, keep your hands off of my plug!

Most of us wouldn't want to become a burden on our loved ones, but what if my loved ones are out of town when this question comes up? I wouldn't want my wife to sacrifice the needs of the school she intends to build to help empower the women of Peru with the money from my future bestsellers. And how can I expect my daughter to drop her culinary consultations with the consulate in Rome just to visit me in my beachfront nursing home in Rio de Janeiro? Having read "The Diving Bell and The Butterfly," I'm telling you no matter what you think of my deteriorated state of affairs, there may be a lot more going on inside my mind than meets the eye.

Actually, I hope I'm wealthy enough to grow my own replacement parts and with the assistance of South American Plastic Surgeons, I'll preserve the illusion of a vibrant seventy year old raconteur, bon vivant and all around dirty old man. Don't you just love men who realize the most attractive thing about them is the size of their wallet? The intellect may lure them in but it's the cash that traps the cuties when you're past a certain age.

There is of course an alternative and as of today, my charming wife still finds me almost fit enough to stand a chance. I could throw caution to the wind, change my eating habits, restrict my overindulgence in every sort of sweet, salty, rich and fatty food, replace half the wine I drink with sparkling water and finally get serious enough about an exercise program for it to become a way of life instead of an annual, month long, vanity fueled and seemingly futile experiment in reshaping my not quite ready for pool time body.

I've climbed the Andes Mountains and danced naked on exotic islands. I've sung with superb musicians and chanted with indigenous tribes. I've dined on sumptuous feasts in upscale homes and top chef restaurants. I married two of the most beautiful women in this world and fathered one incredible child. I've been applauded on stage and in board rooms as an expert on things I consider harmless at best. I've made fortunes and spent them frivolously. I've made friends and kept them for life. I've seen beauty the depths of which can only be reflected in our own tears and all I can tell you for certain is: whether I get myself in fighting shape or not, please don't pull my plug too soon! I can't get enough of this life!

A World Away . . .

I peer into a dense green leafy respite through a warm low lying mist and catch a glimpse of a red bellied warbler gliding in between the dark brown branches. That should cover the cost of any man's passage on the planet for a day, but I've got work to do and bills to pay and other assorted nonsense to pursue.

When did we all get too busy to sit and sip the nectar? I drove alongside people heading to our offices this morning and they couldn't even wait to get behind a desk to start texting, tweeting and arranging for virtual meetings. Breakfast is a drive through burrito with a not too hot cup of Kenyan coffee. Lunch is time to power walk around the parking lot and drive-time home enables us to kill two birds with whatever stones we've got left at the end of another grueling day.

I was somewhere along the Inca Trail, high in the Andes mountains when I came across a young boy sitting peacefully atop a huge boulder, singing to himself as he gazed out upon the valley below. He wasn't startled to see me. I think he must have heard my footsteps long before I got anywhere near him. He smiled and tilted his head a bit as if regarding me with mild curiosity. I said the word for train in Spanish, *tren*, but that didn't seem to register. I made the "whoo whoo" sound while pumping my arm in some childhood imitation of a locomotive and that finally got him excited. He scurried down to take my hand and lead me along a path I never would have found without him.

I wonder what he's up to today. He'd be in his late twenties by now. Does he still have time to sit on top of a boulder and look out over the valley? Or is he too busy raising crops, herding llamas, hustling tourists and struggling to make ends meet? I wonder if he ever went to school. Maybe then he could have gotten a factory job, making shirts for Calvin Klein and LL Bean. He might even have landed a plum job with the American Tobacco company or one of the oil refineries that would pay him enough to marry a cousin's cousin who had moved to the city years ago and could make a home for them in a modest apartment in the suburbs complete with a television, running water, gas stove and refrigerator. Their kids would grow up drinking Inka Cola and going to Catholic School which would cost him half his wages, but they'd be part of the modern world. They could manage hotels when they grow up or even study to become doctors and nurses.

If they did grow up to manage hotels, their hotel chain might even send them back home where they had just built a tourist resort so wealthy people could hike along the Inca trail and go bird watching. If they grew up to be doctors or nurses, they could afford to vacation there.

I picture us sitting on top of that boulder together. Even after all these years, we wouldn't have to say a word. We'd look into each other's eyes and smile sadly before turning our gaze to the valley below.

In Memory of ATC

My pop would have been ninety-one years old today, but even as much as he loved life, he wasn't built to last that long. He was born Anthony T. which stood for Tone, when his father, most likely confused by the question of a middle name, answered the officials with what he intended to call him. He was the third child of Italian immigrants, the first one born in a hospital and raised in Trenton, NJ. He claimed that, as a kid, he had once shined Al Capone's shoes on the corner of Market and Broad. And he remembered a Christmas during the depression, when he and his brothers and sisters each got an orange as a present and considered themselves the lucky ones. Despite growing up in a relatively poor immigrant family during the depression, he became a really good swimmer and diver thanks to the Delaware River and a new state of the art pool, which he was among the first to use at Trenton Central High School. He also developed a life-long love of horses by working as a stable boy at the local armory after school.

He was stationed in Trinidad and Tobago during WWII and developed a modestly successful business there by acquiring local rum for the officer's club and enlisted men alike; applying two distinct labels and price structures to the same basic product. He was an army sergeant but I always pictured him perfectly fitting in McHale's Navy. After the war, thanks to his aforementioned aquatic skills he became a lifeguard on Miami Beach for a little while but eventually came back home to help out his family.

He met my mom in a bar when she was on a date with another guy. Smooth operator that he was, he sort of tripped her on her way to the ladies room and while helping her up, he handed her a matchbook cover with his name and phone number on it, insisting, with a wink, that she had dropped it. She had another date that weekend, but canceled it and called him. My grand mom fell in love with her first and the rest is history. They bought a house in the suburbs for around seventeen thousand dollars, had my brother and then five years later had me to complete the family.

My dad used to manage a small deli like American Store on Market Street before it became the A & P. He turned down the idea of diving into the supermarket business, tried his hand at life insurance and then landed a job in security across the river with U.S. Steel. He worked there for thirty plus years and earned a good living with benefits and a pension but he also took odd jobs everywhere for extra pocket money and to keep us well fed and clothed. He worked the press room at the Trenton Times, drove school buses, pumped gas during the holidays at the Getty Station and taught swimming classes for the "Y" all summer long at three or four local pools. I still run into people everywhere who learned how to swim with him.

I could probably go on for another few hundred pages about him and may have to do that someday, but one thing very few people knew about my pop was how much he loved to read. His favorite books were historical fiction, set in ancient civilizations and he is at least one half of the reason why I became a writer. He was also the best friend I ever had. Thanks Pop—I miss you—today and every other day.

Grace

I'm living proof that most men mature slowly, if at all, and I apologize to anyone who counted on me for anything more than a good time in my teens and twenties. By the time I hit my thirties, you should have known better than to trust me. I may not have been quite as full of myself by then, but I was still more interested in me than anyone else.

God Bless you mom and may He hold you in his arms. You were already an angel on this earth before your maker called you home. I can't begin to count the ways in which you graced my life with your love and kindness, tenderness, laughter and compassion. You were the nearly impossible role model for the woman of my dreams.

Damn you Oedipus for ruining a good relationship. When I was growing up, my mom was a young, vibrant, sexy, intelligent, confident woman who managed a household, put up with her husband's bad habits, encouraged her children's dreams and worked part-time to pay for the special joys in life like summer vacations at the Jersey Shore or toys piled under a Christmas tree.

Even though we talked easily and often, I never got around to telling her how much I admired her strength and appreciated her struggle. I was a selfish and immature, thirty three year old, washed up, would be rock star when she passed away and I wish more than anything in this world she could have lived long enough to see me grow up to be the man that she deserved as a son.

My mom lost her father when she was very young and her mother in her early teens. She was shuttled around from relative to relative to foster home to indentured servitude; sometimes treated with kindness and at other times, not so much. No matter how badly she was taken advantage of, she never turned her back on anyone. It has taken me a long time to realize that she wasn't seeking their approval or afraid of losing them. She was determined to rise above petty problems and show me the strong, compassionate person I could become. My father may have worried that the world would take advantage of me. My mother wanted me to be strong enough to let it.

There are not enough words and phrases in any language to express the love and gratitude I feel towards the woman who gave me this life. All I can say is that thanks to her, I married a woman who is equally incredible and she has graced me with a daughter that has blessed us both. I wish my mom was here to enjoy it with us, because I am on my way to becoming the man she wanted me to be.

A Yankee Jazz Singer in Cuzco

Cuzco sits about eleven thousand feet up in the mountains and your pilot has to navigate between two huge Andean peaks before smacking onto the poorly paved tarmac in a way most foreigners consider bone jarring, as we watch the locals smile, having landed safely.

Using a phrase that has served me well in other Latin American cities, I ask the taxi driver to take me to "the second best hotel in town." That tells him I want something clean and comfortable but I'm not an idiot who will pay top dollar without negotiating. He takes me to the Hotel San Augustin—a beauty and a bargain where I settle in to stay for an indeterminate length of time while I work on my first great American novel.

They serve me Mate de Coca—a tea made of coca leaves to combat altitude sickness. It's not advisable to do much more on your first day than take a short walk on the cobblestone streets. I browse the postcards, Chiclets, candy, roasted pigs, ears of corn and alpaca sweaters plus hand crafted jewelry offered by the local street vendors dressed in their colorful peasant garb. My wonderful good fortune leads me to a Peruvian—Japanese restaurant named Pukaru—that serves one of the best soups I have ever had in my life along with a modest—almost Buddhist dish of rice and veggies that was equally satisfying. I don't know if the place is still there—but it was nearly worth the trip all by itself.

The second day, I make my way to Sacsayhuaman (or as the guides suggest remembering it—Sexy Woman), the ruins of an Incan village in the foothills a few miles outside of town. In addition to the massive stones, so precisely cut they defy you to slide a single sheet of paper in between them and the remnants of ingenious terraced farming techniques that gave water and shade in measured amounts calculated to produce the greatest crop yield on each successive level;

I am shown a curiosity by a young local girl who must have peeked into the very depths of my soul. She introduces me to the speaker's circle which is a group of stones about a hundred pounds a piece and roughly eighteen inches tall by two foot wide. They are set in an oval shape surrounding a soft clay substance she advises me not to walk upon. It's about fifty feet across and yet, as we stand on opposite sides, she whispers and I hear her lovely young voice as if inside my own head, with absolute and perfect clarity. I start to sing softly and feel my own voice amplified from beneath me and inside me in a way that no studio will ever reproduce. A geologist I speak with later explains that the Inca created a natural echo chamber beneath the sacred ground for the purpose of enhancing the speaker's voice from on top of any stone surrounding the circle. They may not have had a written language, but they sure knew their acoustics.

Back at the hotel that night in the bar, restaurant and lounge upstairs, I listen with great amusement to an organist playing Broadway show tunes and thirties and forties jazz standards. In a moment of inspiration, I start to sing along and am invited to stand beside him and entertain the modest crowd. The next night, we are joined by a violinist and a drummer, playing the Peruvian Cajon which is a thin wooden box played bare handed while sitting on top of it. The hotel manager hears I've drawn a crowd—they don't get many Yankee jazz singers in this part of the world—so my room and meals are free from then on—as long as I feel like singing a couple hours every night. It turns into one of the nicest gigs I've ever played.

Tuesday Night Jazz

"Do not fear mistakes. There are none."—Miles Davis.

I was at Monterrey Jazz Festival in the early eighties when Miles held court backstage and I overheard Richie Cole say that no one else from Trenton had made it there that year. I corrected him. He may have been the only one from Trenton onstage that year, but I had certainly made it to Monterrey. That was the first time we met and a rising star can easily be forgiven for not remembering the assistant producer's gopher who chauffeured Freddie Hubbard around and had the honor of giving Sarah Vaughan fresh flowers after a standing ovation. There were tears in my eyes even before she asked me with complete sincerity "was that okay?"

The next time I saw Richie was years later, blowing that beautiful alto sax of his at Joe's Mill Hill Saloon in Trenton on a Tuesday night, sitting in with Tommy Passarella on his Hammond B3 and Cedric Jensen on the drums. I can't remember who else sat in that night, but guitarist extraordinaire Dick Gratton always comes to mind when I think about Mill Hill since he and I played there a few wonderful times. I think we both actually sat in that night because I either played with Tom, Cedric, Dick and Richie or dreamed about it so vividly it's become one of my favorite memories. Either way, I held my own by remembering if you repeat something long enough it stops sounding like a mistake and turns into a direction. That was the accepted corollary to what Miles had to say.

In between the first time I saw Richie in Monterrey and the last time in Trenton, which was quite a few years ago, I got schooled in singing jazz by good tutors in interesting places. I did studio work at Santa Barbara sound and I was Cal Tjader's opening act at La Casa de la Raza. You could even say that Poncho Sanchez punched up my act. Chic Streetman gave me life and performance lessons I'll never forget and the house band at Chico's in Rio de Janeiro along with a vocal group called Cor e' Canto made my songs sound better than I had ever imagined they could. Miami did some nice things for my sound and yet a small home studio in Yardville, NJ with a few good friends and local musicians was one of the most prolific periods in my life and the engineer there had the biggest ears and heart I've ever known.

I haven't played music for a living in years and I don't miss it as a career choice. It only barely paid the bills when I was young and bohemian, but it took me to some breathtaking places in life and introduced me to some incredible people. Tuesday nights used to be a refresher course and gave me the sense of a community of likeminded worldly wanderers. We paused for a moment to bend time to our will and let the music play. There was only one time when I knew I had sung the best I ever could and I'll never forget Sarah Vaughan asking me if what she had done was okay.

Reunion

We remembered each other's faces, but couldn't recall the names. We'd last seen each other in the halls of our high school forty years ago. Some of us had classes together. Some of us had none. Some were reminded of innocent crushes. Others relived more painful crashes. Our lives had moved on without losing the link to a time when we challenged our boundaries. Our minds and bodies were young and energetic then and the future was ours to mold. Now our eyes smiled tenderly into each others admitting we'd all gotten old.

"I'd recognize you anywhere," he said giving her a hug. "Even with the extra thirty pounds," she laughed a little sadly with a voice that had only gotten sexier with age. "I used to have a thing for her," he admitted watching her on the dance floor. "I think I'll take a shot at her. I hear she's single again." "My God that dress looks great on you," one girlfriend said to another. One family friend from grammar school asked about another's older brother.

There were couples who had coupled long ago and had grandchildren filling their hearts. There were some who had lost love to death and divorce and were willing to make new starts. There were spouses, fiancés and faithful friends bellying up to the bar together and swapping stories. There were sadly a few tales of woe, but thankfully more tales of glory.

On the whole we looked pretty good for our age, or any other for that matter. Only a few had gotten thinner, most a little fatter. The men wore suits and sport coats, looking fairly well styled. The women clearly out did themselves, some dressed in seductive smiles. In evening wear and dancing heels they strutted to disco beats and reminded every man with blood in his veins they'd been the keepers of our treats.

Conversations were brief due to time and circumstance. Most had come to dine and drink and do a little dance. We mostly caught up in small talk, giving broad strokes to fill in the blanks. It was heartening to hear how many of us simply wanted to give thanks. We were a large and unruly force back then and we've finally become civilized. Many lead lives of comfort and kindness with dreams almost realized.

The eyes tell the story, when we greet each other through the years. We can see each other's candid smiles and feel each other's tears. We share a depth of experience based upon more than what we went through together. No matter where our lives may lead us, we are truly connected forever.

The Heart of the Matter

Most of my friends have been around the block, some have been around the world. There's a strange event that occurs when men of a certain age gather in social settings with other men who are considerably younger than they are. For lack of a better term, we'll call it "Tall Tale Telling Time" or the 4T Phenomenon for short. It usually consists of drunken recollections, drug induced vagaries, bawdy accomplishments and my personal favorite, adventurous embellishments laced with celebrity encounters.

Every man has almost had a threesome, sighted an enormous snake hiking in the wilds of somewhere, partied with one of the Grateful Dead or a member of the Red Hot Chili Peppers, dated someone who either was or looked like a supermodel, woke up with someone who clearly was not, got stuck in a storm of some sort, drank so much they went blind in one eye, was temporarily convinced of an alien encounter under the influence of illegal substances and knows someone who crossed the Mexican border with ten kilos hidden in their wheel wells.

Rugged manly stuff goes over well and though the teller might have actually been scarred for life, his skirmish with a great white in the waters off the coast of Madagascar will make him a hero over and over again. The guy who saw an actual lion kill an actual anything inspires enough attention from the younger men that they will actually go get a beer for him when he's done recounting it in gory detail. Football injuries are not as big as being gored by a bull, but they'll do in a pinch and garner some respect. Long arduous treks through uniquely isolated or foreign terrain play well as do claims of nights having anything to do with tribal rituals.

Meanwhile back on the dance floor, the women are kicking it old school which means they are drinking champagne and having catty conversations about a woman that isn't there or worse yet, is there but isn't welcome. They talk about their body fat, their booty shake, the makeup tips passed down from one generation to the next, how hot their legs look in high heels, how cleavage makes a man their slave and costume jewelry is getting better all the time. In truth I'm only guessing about their conversation, since I'm out there doing my part in the male circle jerk until we all come together and dance like the wild abandoned natives we wish we still were.

To be fair, this type of behavior is only appropriate at large gatherings. Otherwise, we sit and discuss Euclidian geometry, share quotes by Nietzsche and agonize over how to raise non violent pork for an ethical pancetta, but you already knew that.

I'm guilty of an extremely exciting life; past, present and hopefully future and yet I'm also hopelessly addicted to efforts to make the past sound even more exciting than it was. So for once I'm going to come clean. I did not surf the pipeline at Albocondo, wherever that is. I never got high with the Dalai Lama. My curve ball wasn't as good as I said it was, and I sound like Don Henley, he doesn't sound like me.

R.I.P. ETTA

It was probably one of the wildest nights of my life and yet surprisingly, I've told very few people about it. It's kind of hard to relive a long evening filled with vices too numerous to mention and challenges that were impossible to overcome even though the learning curve got thrown out the window and my street quotient rose substantially from that night forward.

I was in my late twenties, living in Santa Barbara when the phone rang after dinner one night. Greg and Regina owned a recording studio in the foothills and they had a surprise guest who wanted to jam with me. If I recall the invitation it was something along the lines of c'mon over around eleven and don't even think about sleeping until the sun comes up.

This was an eclectic and dynamic duo. He was a couple years older than me; a heavy set white guy dressed in suits most of the time; hustling blues, jazz and R & B demos all over L.A. and if memory serves me well, doing some investment brokering to keep the properties paid. She was a voluptuous young black diva with a voice that knocked the hell out of you, but she was also wild, dramatic and demanding. As intimidating as they could be, I really enjoyed their company and frankly I was too afraid of them to turn down a studio request at that point in my life. You never knew what to expect with them and this turned out to be something I'm glad I didn't miss.

When I got there, they greeted me with great big smiles, shots of hard liquor and lines of cocaine. I had some catching up to do and the guest of honor would be with us shortly. Once we were in the studio, Greg cranked up some rhythm tracks that sounded vaguely familiar, handed me a microphone and told me to start warming up. At best, I was a background singer who could hold my own on the songs I wrote when I couldn't find other people willing to sing them better, but trust me I was no match for who was about to show up.

I heard a low growl that made me shiver. It was the most sensual sound I'd ever heard; catlike, confident and overwhelming. When I turned around I was face to face with Etta James who was ready to tear me apart. I have never met anyone in my life sexier, stronger or nastier than that woman. She challenged me to sing and shout every emotion I had within me. She made me howl notes I never knew I could produce. We sweated out verse after bluesy verse, making it up as we went along. We rocked the house, tore off the roof and shook it til' the break of dawn.

It turned out that her son Dante had been in my songwriting workshops and she wanted to see what I was made of. When the session was over she licked her lips and gave me that famous lascivious smile. "Not bad for a skinny little white boy," she offered and I'll take that to my grave as great praise.

Momentarily Vegetarian

If I mention "fava" beans, many of you will think of having them with "a nice Chianti," like Hannibal Lechter did in Silence of the Lambs. My previous memory of them was tied to my father's description of the driest most bitter and horrible, if at all edible, ingredient his mother ever forced him to eat. Considering the fact that his was a poor Italian immigrant family, I figured this was one food I would never need to get familiar with. If he thought it was horrible, as hungry as they were at the time, then my highly refined TV dinner supplemented and comfort food oriented palate was not going to try them at all. I had enough problems with lima beans, even the green ones in succotash, let alone the brown ones served separately as an unspeakable act of culinary cruelty.

All of that changed last night at the hands of a master chef. Chris Albrecht from Eno Terra in Kingston gave a cooking demonstration at a local event and served an executive salad to thirty or forty of us newly initiated "fans of fava." The beans were so tender and creamy; perfectly balanced by the hazelnut and virgin olive oil dressing over crisp frisee atop a slice of coto and adorned with a good wedge of pecorino romano. Feel free to sing that recipe. Chef Albrecht rocked it and my taste buds were delighted.

The Chef contends that the most important ingredient is the soil in which the plants are grown. Native Americans trace it all the way back to the mood of the farmer when the seeds are sewn. My senses are only sharp enough to recognize the crisp delicious flavors of something freshly picked. The art of arranging edibles for a balance of nutrition, taste and beauty is a devotion worthy of the Gods.

I was a vegetarian momentarily for three years in my twenties. It gave me a chance to expand my working class palate. My mom was a wonderful cook, but I grew up on meat and potatoes or meat and pasta. Luckily, my summers were filled with fresh vegetables and spices from our own garden including incredible jersey tomatoes, tender young zucchini, sweet green peppers, cucumbers, eggplant, garlic and oregano. But that was where the exploration ended. The rest of the year it was French fries and turkey clubs, frozen peas and carrots mixed into chicken ala king over wonder bread toast. I'll never forget how surprised I was that somebody other than Uncle Ben, Rice-a-Roni or the local Chinese restaurant knew how to cook rice.

My vegetarian exploration took place in sunny southern California where I re-discovered artichokes which my grandmother had stuffed and baked. I learned to twice bake a big potato stuffed with broccoli, onion, mushrooms, tomatoes and cheese—no I never went so strict as to cut out the dairy products. We made vegetarian lasagna and pastas with sautéed vegetables. We had rice and steamed veggies or meatless nut loaves sliced like bread and smothered in dark mushroom gravy alongside ears of corn and simple salads. We ate well but I was very thin in those days. The diet coupled with an active lifestyle nearly did me in. I never learned to get enough protein in me, because I hated the thought of fava beans. Maybe it's time to try again?

The Third Act

My first career was in Arts and Entertainment. I was in Southern California, in my early twenties and it's true what they say about Hollywood. The head honchos all realize that sincerity sells and if they could learn to fake that they would. Every waitress is auditioning for a part. Every gas station attendant has a screenplay he's peddling and every plumber, housepainter and limousine driver thinks he should be your agent based on the high level industry contacts he's got. I spent a lot of time at parties with people who were looking for the next big thing. I have to admit, I learned to bullshit like the best of them and it eventually got to the point where none us could tell what was truly worthwhile even if it bit us in the ass and decadence be thy name—it stole a piece of my soul.

Lucky for me, I fell ass backwards into the Arts and Education wing of culture's back lot and met a lot of really dedicated artists, administrators, educators and supporters. I regained a bit of my innocence and spent a few years actually working on my craft. I wouldn't trade those days for anything. They led me to the conclusion that I had earned the right to write.

I pursued art for art's sake for more than a decade and had adventures too numerous to mention in musings as limited as these until I completed the first true opus of my life—a novel hand written on yellow legal pads in the foothills of the Andes. "SongMaker" was the story of all I knew before I reached the age of thirty-something and I'd still like to see it published someday—but something unexpected and miraculous happened when I finished it that changed my life forever and for better. I met my wife, my partner, my reminder of the best this life has to offer. Art could take a backseat to a truer love than I had ever known existed.

When our daughter was born I entered my second career, selling office equipment in Corporate America. My wife never asked me to give up my writing and never complained about what little we had in the way of material comforts or household goods. Instead, she worked side by side with me building a home, nurturing true friendships and providing an education for the light of our lives. I know it sounds crazy, but my writing has flourished over the past fifteen years in ways I would never have believed possible.

Fortunately or unfortunately, I now can say with some certainty that corporate America has stolen a piece of my soul in exchange for the comforts and illusion of stability it has afforded us. I don't regret the experience, but I've gotten about all I can out of it and I'll be moving on in the next few years before my welcome wears out.

It's time for my third act and I can't wait to share it with you. Hopefully, I can combine some of the best elements I've learned and recapture the joy and innocence of creating art and entertainment so those hotshots in Hollywood have something with a Heart and a Soul to sell.

Accounting versus Reckoning

"It's nothing personal. It's just business. You understand, don't you?" Mark Allen Mariner would never be the same. He was unceremoniously pink slipped at fifty seven years of age after thirty-two years spent tallying up receipts for the Baxter Bates Auto dealership in Rapid City. He was an only child and his parents were long gone. He had never married or even dated much for that matter. He was a pleasant person, rather nondescript, who had kept to himself up to this point in time and aside from a voyage he imagined inspired by his own last name he was somewhat short of ambition and not what anyone would have considered an adventurous sort.

The saleswoman told him he looked dashing in the tuxedo he tried on clandestinely. He paid cash and got an extra cummerbund and tie set that matched the patent leather shoes. He had never been to Monaco before, but imagined that was how he should dress at night if he wanted to blend in with the regular crowd. A week ago, he could have fit everything he owned in one suitcase, but he packed two for the trip and took a carry-on along as well.

The over sized cabin on the first class Ocean Liner cost him a small fortune, but since he had never spent a dime on anything more than his very basic needs, he had substantial savings not to mention the retirement fund he was taking with him from his uninformed former employer. By the time they realized the money was gone, he'd be long forgotten. They never would have thought him clever enough to begin with, those oh so greedy salespeople and their co-conspirators in the leasing department.

He didn't start siphoning off a royalty until his seventh year in the money pit. Then one day, a particularly sleazy salesperson bragged about how much he was going to make on a young couple buying their first new car. Mark Allen decided to start the Mariner fund that very week and for the next twenty-five years, he had a small percentage of each salesperson's commission diverted to a separate account under the guise of a transaction fee to cover the cost of title monitoring as a line item buried under title production and title insurance. Since the percentage itself was miniscule and salespeople were used to seeing a range of fees deducted from their paychecks, no one ever caught on and over the years it built into quite a nice little nest egg. The owners just assumed that it was a state tax requirement being big picture thinkers and all. Mark Allen chuckled thinking it was nothing personal, just business.

The fact that he had never driven a car, actually made riding around Monaco in the back of a hired Bentley, fairly natural for our new adventurer. Granted, he was more accustomed to the local bus routes back in Rapid City and the little bit of French he had picked up via tapes in the public library didn't cover topics like how to bet in baccarat or how much to tip a high priced call girl, but he didn't do too badly, all things considered and after a few weeks in town people began to think of him as a resident. His math skills made him a natural at the gaming tables and his modesty kept his win lose ratio well under management's radar. There was a high end auto convention in town after he had been there a year and one of the salespeople thought they recognized him, but by that time his French was fairly decent and the stunning blonde on his arm could never have ended up with the dweeb from the accounting department, could she?

"Brother, can you spare a dime?"

The closest I've ever gotten to panhandling was a weekend I spent in San Francisco back in the late seventies when a buddy of mine opened up his guitar case in front of us at the wharf while we sang and played for whatever change anyone could spare. We actually sounded pretty good and we made something like seventy bucks for a few hours work then we ate and drank like Kings.

I've been down on my luck at times, but never without a roof over my head, a place to sleep and a decent meal. Don't get me wrong, I've been hungry a time or two, but all I ever had to do was work my way out of it and back in those days there was always a job to do if you weren't too picky. Starving artists can't afford to be too picky.

I remember working as a day laborer for a friend of mine who was a plumber out in Southern California. I was digging a trench to hold some pipes he needed to lay for a hillside mansion that overlooked the Pacific. It was a gorgeous place, a sunny day and I didn't mind the physicality of it in my early twenties. I was dark skinned already and working on my tan with a shovel in my hand, making ten bucks an hour. The owner of the Carpentaria estate noticed me and brought me an iced tea. My buddy had warned me not to stop working if I wanted to keep the job, so I wanted to get back to the task at hand after thanking the guy, but he wanted to show me around. I hadn't spoken a word besides mumbling "thank you" for the iced tea, so he couldn't have known anything about me and like I said, I was dark skinned plus I had a dark beard so it's easy to see how he could mistake me for a Latino immigrant. "I used to have a boy like you," he said, "living right here on my estate. Let me show you." He opened the door to a tiny little utility shed hidden behind the main house furnished with a mattress, nightstand and lamp as if he were revealing a sultan's palace. "This could be yours plus food and a hundred dollars a week and all you have to do is help me take care of the grounds. What do you think?"

Luckily the plumber got there in time to save the owner the embarrassment of whatever I might have responded. He shouted at me to get back to work, as if it were my fault, so he could deal with it discreetly. I've met people in my life since then, who would have been grateful for that opportunity. Here in the states, we have very little idea of how poor people can be and once you see it firsthand you can easily understand why so many central and south Americans think of this as the Promised Land.

I've dug ditches, cleaned apartments, bartended; desk clerked, painted houses, spread pitch on rooftops and worked in almost every kind of retail store or hotel you can imagine. I've taught drama and music, written arrangements, been a studio musician, sold door to door, translated books from Spanish and managed to sell millions of dollars worth of office equipment. There is no job beneath me including the one that comes with a palatial suite disguised as a utility shed. There but fore the Grace of God . . . I can sing for my supper and "brother can you spare a dime?"

All in . . .

They tell athletes to leave it all on the field and performers to leave it all on the stage, but you can't expect a painter to use all of his palate at once or a writer to put it all on the page. Sometimes the best and the brightest shine because of what they've left behind.

Nat King Cole could sing like a lark but preferred playing piano when given a choice. It's hard to imagine a song more haunting than Nature Boy in his voice. Picasso painted awhile in blue just to show what he could do, but his Three Musicians played a brilliant rendition based on themes understood by few.

Hemingway had a way with words and used them with great care. Vonnegut rambled until he'd used every syllable and some that weren't even there. Joyce forgot to punctuate but Seurat made his points. Harrison made the guitar weep and someone rolled Marley's joints. Dali dared the hands of time while Cezanne captured Provence. Jimi kissed the skies on fire while Misha made hearts dance.

In literature there are forms such as letters, essays and novellas. In painting there are mediums like acrylic, oil and water. On the stage, the plays the thing unless the players sing. On the field the game's afoot unless someone makes a racquet? I do like the fact that Golf greats win a jacket. But if a Tony is worth its weight in gold aren't paintings worth more when they get old?

In the beginning there was the word and the priests thought it was priceless enough to protect. So how could they have burned all of the Mayan libraries they found in the New World? As far as we know the Incans had no written language, but based on how their neighbor's literary efforts fared when faced with the onslaught of Christian soldiers, it wouldn't surprise me if they hid their writings somewhere.

A novel and a symphony were out for an evening stroll. The literate one wondered For Whom the Bell would Toll. The musical minded measured their progress in counts from one to four, but threw away the meter once he knew the score. The game was tied in the top of the ninth when a referee called fowl. We had no idea who'd won the game until we heard Ginsberg Howl.

I've let my phrases have their way and hopefully amused. I may have wasted precious moments, not the first time I've been accused. Words like notes and brush strokes occasionally need to be aired. Trust me when I tell you, this isn't the worst I've fared.

Someday I'll write my masterpiece in hundreds of thousands of words and someone will have sense enough to listen instead to birds.

The Peacemakers

Isn't it strange throughout our history, how men of peace are so controversial while men of war are so easily understood and accepted? We consider ancient tribes barbaric and yet the forward march of our Christian soldiers that eradicated them is viewed as an almost benevolent force.

The fact that Christ the revolutionary has been co-opted by Evangelical politicians is a prime example of blasphemy in my book. While I have no doubt that his grace lives and breathes in the hearts and minds of countless genuine believers, I find it highly unlikely that he would rest easy with the hypocrisy and intolerance promoted in his holy name by the money makers and power brokers who run massive organizations for the benefit of anyone but the humble.

Gandhi was considered a strange little bugger, who drove the British Empire out of India with a rallying cry of peaceful resistance and non-threatening homegrown industries of modest means that had astounding ripple effects and reverberations which will still be felt for centuries to come. He was also martyred for his efforts and his legacy has sadly devolved into less than diplomatic wrangling over military and industrial supremacy.

We don't actually know that much about Buddha or Mohammad here in the west. The former is frequently thought of as a rotund happy wanderer who somehow managed to get fat as a vegetarian, but then again, that makes sense because we still consider his people inscrutable for the most part. The latter is a highly controversial figure today, after middle-eastern zealots stuck in the middle ages and associated with his doctrine interpreted his instructions as a battle cry that struck at the very heart of our modern world. Of course there is no way to excuse that and I am not by any means a religious scholar, but history tells me that the devil is most likely in the details misinterpreted in the name of personal gain rather than in the holy words so many others find filled with peace and compassion.

Today, we honor Martin Luther King, a man whose oratory skills and empathy for the downtrodden were both rare and inspirational. He was reviled by the great white establishment of his day; hounded for whatever human frailties he may or may not have possessed and assassinated for the courage of his convictions. He paved the way for both Mandela and Obama to walk upon the world's stage as victors on behalf of a people so long oppressed. Thanks to him, we are truly one step closer to a world of greater equality and understanding.

Everywhere in the world today, there are children following in the footsteps of the peacemakers. Blessed be those children for the beauty of their dreams. God grant them strength along with their kindness and compassion. If history tells us anything—they're going to need it.

The Grand Bazaar

A friend of mine just got back from a vacation in Istanbul. I don't get jealous very often and rarely envy anyone, but as she described the Grand Bazaar I could just picture myself smoking a hookah, sipping apple tea and considering a handmade Persian rug. A young barefoot child cautiously slips me a note from the veiled woman who had glanced at me dark eyed and inviting when she refilled my cup. In flowing English script it says to meet her by the well of Allah after the evening prayer. She doesn't dare sign her name, but the carpet seller calls her Jasmine. I conclude my transaction and hurry off to find a tailor who will craft a hidden pocket for the jewels I intend to help her smuggle out of her captor's cache in order to buy her freedom upon my return.

The night is filled with incense. Soft pillows emit the smell of patchouli as I lean back upon them. The water is scented with lavender as she gently washes my hands in between the courses eaten without utensils. Fresh ground lamb is rolled into spicy rice and held together with a mid sized mint leaf. It is followed by a mixture of dates, nuts and honey, layered into a thin pastry covering tender slivers of roasted chicken. She slips me a round red ruby the size of a small Spanish olive and I employ the hiding place with grace while feigning a stretch and yawn maneuver. The emerald and sapphire she presses into my palms with absolute and perfect stealth between the next two courses are the size of a pistachio and fig, both exceptional in clarity and cut but I won't realize that until they have also been released from my secret stash in private, much later that same evening. The piece de resistance is a sparkling white diamond large enough to cause me concern. It's a tear drop shape and warm to the touch as if it held the light of a thousand passionate nights.

I make it across the desert in a caravan and find myself in a small port city. The man in the white linen suit who greets me with the jeweler's loop knows where the bounty came from and doesn't care. It's a small enough sample not to draw too much attention, but of a quality rare enough to fetch a pretty price. We settle on number for the first three pieces to be paid in golden coin and I negotiate a fortune in Damascus silk which will be shipped to me overseas to match the value of the peerlessly bright white tear.

Back in the carpet seller's lair behind the Grand Bazaar, the veiled woman's warden gives me a glance of tempered steel when I broach the subject of her release. If he wants his recompense he cannot admit she has stolen from him since that would require her death. So we haggle over her attributes until I pretend to reach my limit and then allow him to extend it only once and only ten percent more. Any greater discrepancy would have shown one of us a fool and risked revealing the fraud we had agreed upon.

As I helped her and the erstwhile barefoot child board a swiftly departing ship, I pressed the few remaining gold coins into her henna tattooed palm. When I get home, I'll dress my own concubine in the finest Damascus silk.

Hurricane Season

I made my way from Annapolis, Maryland down the intercoastal waterway on a thirty-eight foot all wooden Dickerson sailboat to Marathon, Florida. That could have been a story, all by itself, but we were originally headed to Brazil. We were going to cruise through the islands and then hug the coast of Columbia making our way from Cartagena all the way down to Recife if not Rio de Janeiro. There were two things we didn't count on. First of all our trip got delayed because the captain's girlfriend needed help with her horses back in Colorado. A weekend turned into a week, turned into a month and while I enjoyed playing tennis, spending time with the girl next door and an occasional jazz gig in the keys to keep myself entertained, the weather took a turn for the worse and hurricane season started a month earlier that year. Needless to say, I had a change of plans.

Somehow I ended up in Belize. Belize City was not that appealing even though I stayed at the Fort George which was the best place in town. My first night there, I ran into a retired army general in the hotel lounge and we got to talking about our travels and shared interests. He knew where I belonged at that moment in time and arranged for a driver by the name of Eddie Fisher to collect me the following morning. Eddie drove me a few hours away through the jungles and into the mountains. Just north of the town of San Ignacio, not far from the Guatemalan border, on a hill that overlooks the best little disco in Central America lies Windy Hill Cottages where I would make myself at home.

Bobby Hales is an American expat, stock car turned ambulance driver who met his match in Belizean bride Lourdes at Tulane University's nursing school in good old New Orleans, Louisiana. The two of them married in Belize and on the back of a successful hardware store, built an ever expanding family and an enchanted little resort. I don't know what the hell I had in common with him other than a fondness for alcoholic beverages and an appreciation of home grown weed, but Bobby and I became true and fast friends. I spent my first few days and nights there like every other tourist, enjoying the horseback riding, swimming in clear and natural mountain streams plus visiting the local ruins. At the end of the week when a large group of tourists arrived, they needed the extra bed in my room to accommodate more guests so they invited me to join them in their own house and I became a member of the family. I stayed on about a month, helping them out with tours and bartending to feel like I was earning my keep. When I left for Peru to finish my great American novel, they made me promise to stop by on my way to the bestseller's list.

It was less than a year later, after finishing my research in Peru, not to mention meeting my future wife along the way and drafting my novel in Costa Rica, that I decided to return to Windy Hills for awhile. They say it's something in the Cayo district water that draws you back, but it might have been the Durley's Rum. It's hard to condense all the misadventures that followed, but Bobby and I did manage to embarrass the Prime Minister at a bridge dedication in a small village when we showed up alongside him drunk on national television, arm in arm with local hookers. We also flew hot young tourists out to the islands on puddle jumpers, drunk alongside a former CIA pilot and offended everyone from the Catholic priests to the British soldiers at homes and taverns across the nation. Sometimes you really just can't avoid the hurricane, no matter which way you turn.

The Next Frontier

I used to manage a resort in Belize, Central America. It was in the foothills of the Maya Mountains a few miles away from the Guatemala border or "en la frontera" as they say in Spanish the third most popular language in a country the size of Massachusetts with fewer people than there are in the city of Boston.

English is the official language, owing largely to the fact that this was once called British Honduras after the Brits stole it from Guatemala blocking off their access to the Atlantic and starting a never ending feud. It has only been independent since 1981 and when I was there in 1989 and 90' it still felt like the wild, wild, west. There was even a group of Texas businessmen who called themselves the Belizean Millionaires Club. You had to have lost at least a million to be able to swap stories with them. I eavesdropped.

I was interviewed by Francis Ford Coppola who has a really upscale resort about twenty miles away from the modest one I managed and there is a British naturalist style place straight out of National Geographic in between the two. Windy Hills was a comfortable cottage industry built upon the principle that tourists would pay a hundred bucks a night to sleep under a thatched roof. After a day of horseback riding, hiking, swimming or visiting the local ruins, all we had to do was feed them a decent meal and pour them some good local rum. The spirits of the jungle did the rest. It didn't hurt that we were close enough to a town for them to find us and just far enough away to make them feel like they had gotten out into the wilds.

The resort was staffed by mainly Spanish speaking maids and gardeners, but Carmela, who ran the kitchen and Theo her husband who was a former soccer star and current tour guide, spoke the second most popular language: Creole-patois with a hint of Garifuna.

It's an African inspired French derivative or maybe the other way around, but whatever it is, it's hard to follow until you've been there awhile. Luckily, I caught on quick enough to avoid becoming a US Passport for Carmela's stunning and statuesque eighteen year old daughter who took aim at me before we'd even met. It would have been a shotgun wedding, but I resisted her offer to teach me their tongue in favor of saving mine.

I got along famously with the Brits and Lebanese who shared most of the nation's wealth along with the few American ex-patriots who had the stamina needed to survive. I probably could have gotten into business with one of the ruling class families, although they all thought I was too easy on the Spanish speaking help. At least they weren't trying to get me to marry one of their daughters.

One fine old Lebanese gentleman heard I was going to marry a woman from Peru and he told me it was "good to improve the breed." Turns out he was constantly "improving" the Guatemalan population by sponsoring young girls he met in villages nearby the lumber camps he used to own. The west was probably quite different than the way we have imagined it. Belize certainly taught me a thing or two.

SongFactory

I had just started teaching drama classes in the local Santa Barbara county schools under the auspices of La Casa de la Raza, funded by the California Arts Council and National Endowment for the Arts, when a group of students at an Alternative School came up with something new they wanted me to teach. Apparently, being so close to Hollywood, they had already seen just about every kind of drama and acting class known to man, but one of them had heard from her parents that I was a local singer songwriter and she convinced a few others that I should teach them how to write songs.

The only way I ever figured out how to teach songwriting was by writing songs together in groups both large and small. It's actually very easy if you have no expectation of penning the next "Bridge over Troubled Waters," and the more you write, the more you learn about how to do it. During the first year, I took part in creating at least a dozen decent ditties and over the next couple years I learned to get myself out of the process more and more so the budding composers could get more involved in their own creations.

The program got pretty popular around town and the local news decided to do a five minute segment in one of my classrooms at the end of their show one night. As luck would have it, Jane Fonda lived nearby and happened to be watching the news that night. She and her husband, Tom Hayden sponsored a children's summer camp on their ranch and were always looking for ways to improve upon the already creative and versatile arts and outdoor programs they offered, so she had her staff get in touch with me. Shortly thereafter, I started offering SongFactory at Camp Laurel Springs in the beautiful Santa Barbara hills. It was an incredible experience in a wonderful place with delightful people and I stayed there for five summers.

At the start of the fifth year, Jane finally approached me to tell me how many good things she had heard about my program. I say finally, because I'd watched so many other people bug her about their pet projects over the years that I never had the nerve to bother her with mine. But once she opened the door it all poured out about the album I wanted to produce of songs written by the kids with them doing the singing, backed up by top notch musicians. To my never ending surprise she agreed, we hugged, signed a deal and I went about recording an album.

There were so many incredible people involved in that production, I could never begin to name or thank them all for everything they did. The album was critically acclaimed and if I do say so myself, artistically uplifting. It really was true to what the kids wanted to express. Unfortunately, the talent agencies, record companies and legal entities conspired to kill any chance of it getting distribution and I'm sure I wasn't the only heartbroken songwriter involved. I have no doubt there were things I could have done to help it reach a wider audience, but I never planned on creating another version of "Menudo," "Up with People" or the Backstreet Boys anyway. I hope the people involved, particularly a couple thousand kids who took the workshops enjoyed what they did and maybe someday one of them will write something we'll never forget.

Archetypes

I grew up in the kind of neighborhood where most of the men wore uniforms to work. Mr. Alito lived a couple blocks away. He was the father of a future Supreme Court Justice, wore button down shirts with knitted ties and smoked a pipe. We didn't know what he did for a living, but we knew he was important. Carl and Lillian Karlberg, Skip and Carla's parents, moved from next door to a bigger house on the corner with a pool. He was white collar, after all—protestant I'm pretty sure, although he did design the addition to Our Lady of Sorrows Catholic Church when I was just a kid. That plus the rumor that he and his wife had once socialized with Einstein made them a little upper crust and the job title architect didn't hurt. I actually saw him go out in a dinner jacket once, so he had to be really cool to pull that off.

Years later, I met a lovely draftsperson named Yuth, from Indonesia I think. She volunteered at the Trenton Film Festival before that wonderful annual event faded to black. She worked for a well known firm in Princeton and practiced what she described as "Architorture;" drawing uninspired utilitarian boxes to house the proletarian tastes of NJ's Pharmaceutical Industry and the rarely ever changing landscape of what passes for trendy retail outlets in the suburbs. I got the impression she had gotten into her field to create sweeping, inspired designs and found out the hard way that the bulk of what gets built does little to fuel a creative spirit.

I'm guessing that my love of architecture started when I moved out to California in my early twenties. I actually lived in an incredible modern redwood and glass ranch house in a canyon in Montecito for awhile and was within hiking distance of beach front places that were featured in Home and Garden, as well as the glossy, impressive Architectural Digest itself. A brief trip to Barcelona cemented my taste for modern, especially when you can find it built near the ruins of equally impressive ancient civilizations: Archeology and Architecture—what a lovely field of research to explore. Throw in a dash of Anthropology, hit me with a little Art for good measure and serve it all with an authentic dish of Cultural and Culinary diversity and I'd be set for a lifelong course of study.

I grew up in a two bedroom cape cod with one bathroom, a back porch I like to pretend I helped my dad build and a partially finished basement. We had a truck garden at the end of our driveway for summer vegetables and a nice back yard complete with a cement grill, croquet set and a badminton net. We were only about seven miles away from the impressive gothic churches and halls on Nassau Street in Princeton. We were only about five miles from the Quaker and Mason landmarks of Trenton. But my love of architecture didn't even start until I moved out to California in my early twenties. I don't blame my parents. They gave me the best of everything they could ever get their hands on and they tried to give me a glimpse of what was beyond their pay grade by sharing their love of reading. I just think it's kind of sad that even though my grandfather was a stone mason who built some of Trenton's finer residences back in the early twentieth century, his children never got to know the kind of craftsmanship and beauty the wealthy people who employed them enjoyed.

Only in America

I've traveled a little bit and even lived in a few other countries for awhile, but there are so many amazing things about this nation of ours that I will always be proud to call it home. For me, it starts with the notion that there are truths we hold to be "self evident." Thank you Mr. Franklin for insisting they were not to be considered sacred and God given, but defended instead against any and all incursions upon whatever true liberty the mind of man is capable of producing. That single brilliant edit enables us to disagree with whatever our fellow man may believe while defending his right to believe it with our very lives.

The truths themselves are a marvel of compassionate philosophy: that all men are created equal and endowed by our creator with the inalienable right to life, liberty and the pursuit of happiness. If only we were all men of goodwill we probably could have left it at that. But the lawyers took over and from that point on we've been codifying, qualifying, amplifying and diluting our rights and our happiness ever since at the expense of the many for the benefit of the few. So what's a poor boy to do? Except to sing in a rock and roll band. Leave it to a British rocker to inspire my rebellion with an anthem to a street fighting man.

Only in America can you quote a French atheist at a graduation ceremony for obedient pet owners held at a Buddhist retreat. You can chant Gregorian, chart Pythagorean, map Magellan and mime Marceau. You can dance a Cha Cha, sing a Samba, paint pointlessly and deify a donut if you like. You can build a business upon edible fashion. You can study the effects of fusion and fishing. You can spend your life devoted to a dollar or work to fulfill what helpless children are wishing. The path you pursue is yours to choose. The promise of America is that the choice is yours.

Time has taught us that life does not come with guarantees; death and taxes aside. You pay your ticket and you take your chances for as long as you can hang on the ride. Here in the still young US of A we've been taking a lot of abuse lately. We're the occupying army against brutal dictatorships people begged us to help them overthrow. We're the guys that gave them billions to rebuild, but now we have the nerve to try and tell them how to spend it. We're the ones who showed people how to live in freedom and it looks like there is no way to end it.

What we lack in culture, we borrow freely and imitation is the sincerest form of flattery. What we make is revolutionary and we need to continue believing in our better selves to keep that dream alive. We discovered electricity and invented the light bulb; modern communication would not exist without us. Our unions were among the first in the world to protect the rights of children and we share our wealth with every other nation on the face of this earth. It's time we stopped feeling guilty about the good fortunes of our birth and started taking care of our own. We may not have achieved all we're capable of yet, but look how much we've grown.

Univision

They just elected a new president in Peru. A leftist populist former friend of Chavez, he was nonetheless the favorite. It was a runoff between him and the daughter of a former Japanese president who had left the office in disgrace and came back to serve his time in prison. You can't make this stuff up.

Peru's economy has been growing steadily for the past seven years due primarily to an increase in mining. Their once exceptional seafood industry has also finally recovered from the years of Russian and Japanese rape. You would think the cocaine business would still be good, but the truth is Peru never has made as much on the raw product as it's neighbors make processing and trafficking in it. I always thought their future would be in both manufacture and tourism. They've got a skilled and willing labor force and more beautiful sights than you could ever imagine. Sadly, the rest of the world discovered their minerals and natural resources long ago and ever since the Spaniards first ruined the place over gold; others have followed in their footsteps only pausing long enough for modern treasures to be discovered and then plundered again and again.

I remember years ago a few well to do Latinos explained to me how you could tell what was going on in Venezuela by watching the Miami Skyline. If a populist government was elected, there would be more skyscrapers going up because the rich Venezuelans would flee. Chavez, of course changed the playing field by changing the constitution so he can stay in office as long as he likes. The rich people left Caracas long ago and they have spread throughout half of Florida, by now. If there had been a hard core military running the show, then Miami would have been on it's own, since the rich would have been protected enough (or could have bought enough protection) to invest in their own backyard. That may just be a strange rationale for what South American's like to call a "mano duro" or heavy hand. They point to the success of Chile ever since Pinochet handed over power and many openly express the crazy belief that other Latin American nations would eventually benefit from that same type of brutal regime.

Speaking of Chile—there was an earthquake there yesterday that I wouldn't have known about if it hadn't been posted on Facebook by a friend in France. We North Americans know so little about what's going on in our own hemisphere. Brazil is booming by the way. They are building at a fever pitch in anticipation of a World Cup tournament and the chance to host the Olympics. They are making deals directly with China and busting to play a bigger part on the world economic stage. If you think Peru and Chile have resources, you wouldn't believe what lies deep in the Amazon jungle.

Whoever makes our foreign policy had better start looking south of the border soon. We can't just continue the conga line by hosting fashion shows and promoting the latest daring bathing suits from our less inhibited neighbors. We need to take these people and places seriously before they wake up and start laughing at us.

To Have & Have Not

Well it's official. According to the AARP I'm an old white man. Unfortunately, I got here a little too late to join the good old boy's club and take advantage of the spoils afforded that dying breed over the past few hundred years. Now we eye each other with suspicion wondering what skeletons are in each other's closets before we calculate an approach based upon potential connections and mutual distrust. We've stockpiled a host of politically correct assumptions we can revert to instantaneously if necessary and we rarely venture more than we can afford to lose.

We're on the verge of a complete socio economic upheaval wherein democratic ideals pay full lip service to whoever can afford them and the complexion of your neighbors will have very little to do with their financial flexibility. For that matter, their sexual preferences, religious practices, ethnic mix and level of education will all take a backseat to their earning power. Welcome to a world of haves and have-nots; the last taboo will send us back to lepers and untouchables before too long. We've proven that we need someone to pick on or at least someone we can lord our superiority over after all. When we can no longer base that on the once undeniable old white man standard, we'll have to look for another way to designate and denigrate those less fortunate than our almighty selves.

What is it about compassion that takes so long to breed? Is it because it's free and therefore hardly worth the trouble to acquire? Is it because anyone can cultivate it—with or without the proper education, registration, reservation or restriction and the only dictum ruling it is dedication to a fair relation to one another that can't be controlled by cost? You win it without anyone having lost? How's that even possible?

Free thinkers are not that easy to find. Most of them mind their own business and keep their revelations to themselves lest someone else profit from them at the expense of the ideal. Frankly it boggles the mind.

So I pull up to the pearly gates in the back of a chauffer driven limo and I'm greeted by a stunning, statuesque blonde in a see through Grecian gown. She's got those dark brown Brooke Shields eyebrows that make her emerald green eyes sparkle and I know she knows I'm blown away. It takes awhile before I realize that Mother Theresa has been standing beside her all along. "Oh Shit," I think. Is this another test? The choices were rarely this obvious in life as I knew it, but it's pretty clear how I'd prefer to spend eternity. My old man pulls up driving Jesus in a jeep and tells me to hop in. "Relax," he tells me no one's out to get you anymore. "We were just fucking with you anyway."

Joseph Campbell said to Jump!

It's hard enough to take a step in the right direction sometimes, let alone a leap of faith. An unofficial survey of a hundred friends would likely reveal that only five percent of the people you know love what they do for a living. Here in the land of good and plenty, a substantial number of people are satisfied that their job is tolerable, mildly rewarding and even occasionally enjoyable, but those who actually have a passion for what they labor at are very few and often learn the hard way that it's best to keep quiet about it. The quickest way to make enemies is to let the world know how blessed your life is. People can't help but try and find fault with anything that looks too good to be true.

We rationalize staying in a dead end job because we imagine that our only other choice would be to have no job at all. We put up with a mounting host of indignities and surround ourselves with ever deepening moral and ethical dilemmas in order to put gas in our cars and afford the toys and trinkets that help us forget what we sold out for in the first place. Our once fervent dreams become vague memories of something we had the nerve to think we could have done. Our prized possessions vie to take the place of the accolades we wish we had fought harder for and won.

Every single one of us knows that the things worth having don't come easy. Only a few are strong enough to stay the course. It is a long, winding, dangerous, deceptive, challenging even torturous road with pitfalls far too numerous to avoid them all, but the alternative is not worthy of the investment it requires. What profit a man if he gain the world at the expense of his own soul?

A long time ago, a potential investor offered to produce my first recording in exchange for fifteen percent of everything I would ever earn. That was fifteen percent of everything, I would ever earn at anything, not just the recording he was going to cough up the money for. When I challenged him, he became magnanimous in retreat and I walked away from something I thought I had wanted badly for the first of many, many times to come.

A dear friend recently reminded me that I had paid me some dues and deserved to hold my head up any way I wanted to. He may never know how much I appreciate the encouragement. You have to kiss a lot of frogs to find one who has the golden goose by the balls tight enough to squeeze out a chance to ride the painted pony off into the sunshine of your love. No it don't come easy, but it's still one hell of a trip.

Bonfire

I'm a city boy at heart, but there is still something primal about a fire pit in the great outdoors. It soothes the soul, calms the nerves and awakens the senses all at the same time. The crackle of sap from wood too green to burn evenly; the flicker of a flame as it lashes a log so lightly you wouldn't think it capable of doing it any harm; the warm earthy smell of burning sage or the barbecue smoke of a hickory oak. Fire at night fans the appetite for food, fraternity or fooling around.

It's easy to understand why we associate fire with food. In every village ever known to every tribe that ever thrived, our earliest meals were cooked over burning embers. We stewed roots and vegetables; roasted fish and animals; baked grains and berries into everything from a peasant's gruel to a king's feast. We discovered the very flavors of our earth and started to combine them in the endless ways with which we not only learned to fill our bellies, but developed our palate and enriched our existence far beyond survival and subsistence, taking it into the realm of art.

The brotherhood we feel beside a bonfire that lights the night is also rooted in our ancient past. This was the end of every day when we shared whatever we had. The warmth provided by the burning wood, could easily relax a people enough to associate that same warmth with the humanity around them. Praise was offered for the source of our food and for those who had prepared it. Pipes were filled with sweet smelling herbs, then lit and passed around to commune with the spirits of our ancestors. The smoke gave way to song and dance as we digested our meals and allowed our bodies to express our appreciation for all we had been given.

Once we had awakened our body's self awareness through gifts made whole by the fire, the flame took on a sensual aspect and led to a greater appreciation of the bodies of others. The dance became an invitation to an even more primal expression of the joys inherent in our coupling. It's highly doubtful that our species would have survived had it not been for date nights inspired by communal conflagrations. Granted, there were fewer distractions in those days, but our great, great ancestors might have been too tired from their hunting and gathering to exert more energy on anything if it weren't for the enticing nature of the flames that lit their libidos.

I've had the great pleasure of a few good campfires in my life. As a child, we roasted hot dogs and marshmallows in our own backyard. As a young man, I stood many times beside what you would have to describe as blood brothers in pure fraternal joy, marveling at the beauty of nature all around us. As a matter of fact, I had that same experience recently with two wonderful friends at a picnic by a lake. I do have to admit, that as much as I enjoy the fraternity of good men, and these were two of the best, I wouldn't mind a few writhing, dancing naked women at my next bonfire. Just saying . . .

First, Do No Harm . . .

One of my best friends is a racist homophobe. I'm a multi-cultureless drama queen so I guess that balances the scales. I'm entirely hetero in case that matters although in deference to my more metro amigos I did have a great mani and pedi for my birthday. Back in my Hollywood days that was considered proper grooming and not too far from macho to stray if you wanted to project the image of a leading man. Of course back in those days you never knew who was straight, gay, bi, tri, or anti-sexual and it really didn't matter as long as one of you had a connection to an up and coming star you could all hitch your wagon to. Fame was the drug of choice and fortune smiled upon anyone associated with it in the form of limos, private planes and weekends in Palm Springs with spa treatment for the ingénues and entourage alike. It might be hard to believe, but that eventually gets boring and in between the snorting and the whoring, not a whole lot of anything with value can be found.

I try to take people on their own terms as individuals without categorizing and limiting the potential for what they might have to share, let alone looking at them as a meal ticket or a lift up whatever ladder we're on at the moment. The Spanish say you should treat those beneath you as if they were supremely important and those above you as if they were your equal. That way you surround yourself with people eager to support you and others who are not surprised to see you standing at their door. I've seen it work in business and I'm sure it works for social climbing in aristocratic circles, but then I'm content to amuse myself by captioning as much as I can from the sidelines. I no longer play the game.

So what does a somewhat socially adept and experienced ne'er do well do with all the irony in life? Observe, enjoy, smile, laugh, comment, capture, write about it, rinse and repeat. I'm in the process of becoming what I always wanted to be—me.

The Buddhist parables tell us not to seek fame, but the western world prizes it above all else. A rich man can't fit through the eye of a needle but he can sleep on silk sheets, hand sewn with the highest of thread counts. A healer's first responsibility is to do no harm because the road to ruin is paved with good intentions. "A writer takes his pen to write the words again, that all is fair in love . . ." Thank you Stevie Wonder . . . I wonder what I would have done without you in my life. It wouldn't have sounded half as nice.

Barnyard Battles

We got us a bumper crop of prairie oysters this year and one a them fancy little holistic cafés is sautéing them up as fast as you can say hold the Dijon mustard for the steak, Diane. Pigs out back struck a motherlode too and we're damned near hip deep in truffle oil. All we need is a little bit of orange zest and we can smoke the competition at this year's culinary challenge.

Hank's planning on serving up his 2020 chili con carne. That's the year his barn burnt down and he saved some of them burnt cedar shavings to sprinkle into the slow cook crock pot his grandma used to win the battle back in the 90's. He made sure I got a plank or two for salmon season cause' he knows I get weak in the knees for pink on the plate.

Mindy Crocker's most likely gonna fricassee again. Cain't hardly blame her. She's got the sweetest little game hens you ever tasted. I just hope she don't go mixing Lemberger with her butter sauce this year. She nearly ruined her dish last time she tried that. I keep trying to tell her to stick with a burgundy or a Bordeaux, but she insists the local legend has got itself a pungent finish that should work well with the roasted birds. Smells too strong for me, but then I like more subtle fare than she usually puts out.

Kitchen tent's going up a week ahead of time so we can each plan a fire pit and racks as we see fit. After last year's mishap, Carlton don't want to take no chances. Poor widow Wilson barely got a dime for Chet's best recipe. Grilled coyote don't sound like nothin' hard to do, but very few people know how to braise it like old Chet did, God rest his garlic loving soul.

I'm going old school this year with corn fed tenderloins and fresh herb stuffing. Even though I got me a truckload of truffles, I'm not gonna resort to drizzling on the brown for the gold. I know one of the judges got a sweet spot for liquid smoke, too, but I'm becoming something of a purist in my old age. Hell I'm even thinking of burning a little bit of sage in between my appetizer and my entrée to make sure they've cleansed their palettes good and thorough.

I heard some Johnnie come lately plans to show up with a microbrew infused buffalo burger and a side of Asian slaw. I don't know where the hell he thinks he is, but this ain't no gathering of amateurs. This here is the Best in County Barnyard Battles and the top prize is a contract with Kraft to design gourmet meals and sauces for the people too far from the farm or as we like to call them—city folk.

Sharpen your knives and work your magic. May the fresh chef win!

A Summer Camp in Maine

I'm afraid I don't know any more about the debt ceiling than I do about the killing floors. I may not be very savvy when it comes to economics or slaughterhouses, but I'm quite adept at imbibing cool drinks and telling tall tales. So pour one of your favorite beverages and find yourself a comfortable place to sit while I spin the story of one summer I spent in the woods near Auburn, Maine.

I was in my early thirties and had recently returned to New Jersey from the Hollywood wars with only a few minor flesh wounds. I wasn't quite ready to ride the great white way but nor was I far enough out to pasture to consider herding the little ones into commercially viable variations of "Menudo," for the benefit of my would be backers who suggested I follow that formula while I still had bridges left to burn.

Somebody who knew somebody heard I was available and looking to get out of dodge, so they offered me a cabin on a lake at an upscale tennis camp serving the teenage children of the uber riche from New York, France and Spain. The American kids who attended were new money trust fund future fans of Glee who had seen all the latest Broadway shows staying in their parent's cramped Manhattan apartments roughing it a bit compared to their usual life on the compound. The Spanish boys were handsome long haired soccer stars naturally devoted to a life in the arts since they could spend hours on end making copies of the Picasso's hanging on their parent's walls. The French girls were beautiful, worldly and dangerous. Their parents owned the world's most famous vineyards. Their weekly allowances were more than most people made in a year. They snuck into the counselor's quarters uninvited smelling of beer and cigarettes, begging them not to tell anyone, promising another rendezvous if one was willing to share their dramatic little secrets.

I held classes every morning on an outdoor stage and coached would be singers, actors and even dancers on how to create their own unique performance pieces. It was actually a very lovely way to spend a summer. I played tennis every afternoon; often with one of the precocious French girls I learned to befriend and confuse by gently rejecting her amorous advances. The Spanish boys would tell me later I should make her my muse and the Americans wanted to discuss how it compared to Nabokov's "Lolita."

The people who owned the camp knew pretty quickly that I wouldn't be back for another year. We kept a safe distance from each other. They applauded the performance pieces as if avante garde was what they had wanted all along. I tried to ignore their strange little competitions that fed some teams steak and lobster while others ate franks and beans.

At the end of the summer, I received a heap of praise and a ton of cash in tips from the visiting parents whose children had credited me with changing their very lives. I took off on a sailboat trip along the Intercoastal that fall, heading for South America with the water sports counselor who turned out to be a cantankerous captain, even if he was a somewhat kindred spirit; but that's another story for another time.

Here's To Tomorrow

If this was my last day on earth, but I couldn't tell anyone, what would I have done differently? I think I would have woken up to a jazz station playing something just a tad bit funky to lift the eyelids. I would have taken time to brew a better cup of tea and sat long enough to enjoy it face to face with my wife and daughter over their coffee and orange juice respectively. Oh how nice it would have been to sit and sip together on the back deck in the pale early morning light, watching that cute fat little bunny rabbit that likes to hang around in our backyard.

I still would have driven my daughter to school, but I might have done it a little more slowly, changed the route and asked her a few more questions about the upcoming Junior Prom she'll be attending this coming weekend. Tell her how beautiful I know she's going to be and how lucky this punk ass kid is that she agreed to go with him. I don't really know him—neither does she for that matter—it's kind of a blind date set up by one of her best girlfriends at another school in another town. They're double dating and the other girl's stepmom is super Italian, hyper protective and I'm good with that. I trust my daughter and I'd let her know it—while I reminded her not to trust any boy under the age of say 90 to have anything other than sex on his mind almost constantly. I'd have to leave her prepared if I knew I was going soon. She still kisses me on the cheek every morning when I drop her off and I figure that's about the best send off I could ever ask for from this life—so we're good there.

Since I'm not allowed to tell anyone, I guess I'd have to make an appearance at my office. I'd sit at my desk pretending there was work that mattered and maybe try my hand at one last poem in honor of the view outside my window that leads into the woods.

I think I'd sneak out for lunch with my wife. I know what you're thinking and that's not a bad idea, but just watching her across the table at a Chinese buffet is almost as good. My God, those tender loving eyes could melt a man if he looked too deeply in them. I'd let her ramble on about this girlfriend's problem and that one's newest grandchild and how the other day a teacher told her she was the best substitute they'd ever had in this district and it would only be a matter of time before they found a permanent position for her. She'd laugh that I hadn't heard a word about the latest cosmetic or fashion bargain she found. She'd ask me about my work and then quickly change the subject to some brain teasing metaphysical challenge based on National Geographic or the Discovery Channel. Then she'd remind me that I still needed to make up my mind about attending a party she had already committed us to three weeks from now. I'd tell her I had to get back to work, just so I could get a hug and kiss goodbye.

With only a little bit of time left, I'd sneak out of town and head down to the beach. I would want to see the ocean and sing a favorite song before my light goes out. If I haven't left things in order, I know that I have friends and family who will take care of the most important things. The most important thing I could ever have done was to let them know I loved them and I like to think I've done the best I could on that score. I'd be off to see more miracles than we can imagine in this life and I'd be paving the way for those I loved and had to leave behind. I'm so happy for another day, I think I'll try and make the most of my tomorrows.

Feliz Cinco

The best job I ever had in my life was at La Casa de la Rasa in Santa Barbara, California. I was in my early twenties and I taught creative writing through a community outreach program to the local schools, working with a team of like minded young artists for pennies, but able to utilize this beautiful facility for shows and concerts under the tutelage of a few fantastic muralists and poets who cared deeply about their community.

Every Cinco de Mayo, we opened La Casa up to the public for a free meal and put on an incredible days worth of shows for the whole family. One of those multitalented muralists manned a grill filled with his specialty; chicken marinated in tequila and lime which he had paid for out of his own pocket. A handsome Latino poet manned the bar and kept the Miller Lite flowing since the local distributor was nice enough to donate a keg or two for the occasion. Four Chicano grandmothers took turns keeping a steady supply of salads and fresh hot tortillas coming out all day long and the rest of us served the tables or entertained the guests while they ate. It was such a heartwarming experience to see people from every strata of Santa Barbara society from dishwashers and gardeners with their wives and kids all dressed up, to real estate moguls, local celebrities and politicians all gathered in celebration of their heritage. I miss that place and all it stood for, plus all that I experienced there. We had a true sense of community based on cultural exchange and artistic expression. There was ballet folklorico, teatro campesino, blues shows, jazz shows, reggae and Mexican dances where I bartended. There was children's theatre and local band nights plus classes, showcases, a library and even a free clinic for awhile. The people who founded this place really had their hearts in the right place.

I'll never forget when my father visited and spoke Italian with an old Mexican caretaker who swore my father must have come from Durango because they got along like old childhood friends. And then one night I had the greatest shock of my life when the father of one of the muralists from Durango came for a visit and he was an absolute doppelganger for my father even when he stood three feet away from me. He scared the living hell out of me when he used my father's voice to speak to me in Spanish.

Over the years, I've had lots of tender times with good friends from diverse cultural backgrounds and they tend to happen on the spur of the moment. At the moment, we don't have a place, other than facebook, the Princeton Library and a couple of local bars where we can congregate for community events. We're a bit more fragmented and even segregated by the economics of our chosen entertainments. I enjoy a mix of people whose only common thread is an appreciation of their differences. Oh well, better to build upon what we have than to curse a cautious climate.

Tomorrow is "Cinco de Mayo" and I'm heading into NYC early to get the party started. I'm in the mood for a little celebration, a little remembrance of days gone by and a cheer for good things yet to come. It's about time to bend over and shake a tail feather . . . Tequila! Mix my margaritas with Reposado 1800 and pass around shots of chilled Silver Patron! Alright—now throw in a gluten free beer! What? I'll have to explain that some other time. I'm not going there today.

Concert for the Moons

I don't recall much exposure to fine art as a child and I could never pull off a stick figure let alone stay within the lines. My older brother painted a beautiful Japanese style floral water color in high school that seemed to come out of nowhere and remains surprising to this day. My father once lent a starving artist a few bucks and got a painting of Trenton's skyline in the 1950's as seen from across the Delaware for collateral. My brother has that museum worthy piece today along with a pair of silver diver's lamps that were as close as I ever got to sculpture as a kid. They were supposedly made from metals our uncle salvaged at the bottom of the black sea.

During high school, I admired the art students with their beatnik cool and had a secret crush on two or three of the girls who painted the sets for the musicals. I enjoyed my time in the chorus, but would rather have been backstage. Unfortunately I had no technical skills to draw upon and audio visual equipment might as well have been Greek to me. I would have been better equipped to understand it if it was. Language was always my go to gift.

During my own bohemian days in Southern California, a good friend, who just happened to be from my hometown in New Jersey, showed me a pen and ink drawing he had done that had a greater impact on my life than he could ever have imagined. It was called "Concert for the Moons," and though I haven't looked upon it in thirty plus years, I can still feel it today. It had a jazz age sense of elegance but didn't take itself too seriously. Its lines were clean, confident and smooth without having to brag about it. It was musical and lyrical, whimsical and sexy, sophisticated, cartoonish and somehow otherworldly. It actually woke me up at night and drove me to compose a companion piece of instrumental music. I only managed to craft ten minutes worth of movements before daily life intervened and I haven't gotten back to it in years, but as crazy as it sounds I can still hear the full symphony it inspired and truly hope to find time to construct it someday.

That one drawing coupled with my high school infatuation for the girls who painted sets was enough to open me up to some of the most beautiful afternoons of my life, spent in private collections and public museums communing with the masters of real, surreal, impressionistic and impassioned works that enrich our lives like gifts from gods. Many of you will understand how the Grounds for Sculpture in my hometown is not only a place of inspiration but a source of pride and connects me to the Sistine Chapel, Madrid's Prado, New York's MOMA and Philadelphia's Museum of Art, The Smithsonian in DC and a thousand other galleries around the world. These sacred spaces echo earth's natural wonders and provide a place for me to worship what I believe.

I went to a Van Gogh exhibit this past weekend and was surprised to find out how much he loved the Oriental Style of painting. In fact, one of his works was a stunning example with Almond Blossoms against a blue background. My brother's version was black branches with pale yellow flowers, but I have to tell you there was something special about it to me. I hear Vincent's brother was a big fan of his, too.

The Seventies

There was a Greek deli on the corner that made an incredible sandwich. I can still remember the taste of lean salty meat and mild white cheese with thin slices of cucumber on a soft torpedo roll drizzled with rich virgin olive oil and sprinkled with fresh herbs. It was amazingly light and delicious as long as you ate it quickly. Otherwise, the oil leaked and the roll got soggy, the cheese slipped and slid and the salami lost its flavor. This was not a food to savor, but a delectable treat nonetheless.

We grabbed one or two of these tasty time bombs with a bottle of water and a bag of chips, then headed to a nearby park behind the Santa Barbara County Courthouse. There we would sit and ruminate for hours on the state of the arts and the role of the artist, the meaning of life and the madness of man, the beauty of nature, her power, our passion, the flowers, the fates, the fusion, the fashion. What wonderful heady days we shared, there among the landscaped gardens in our overpriviledged slice of life.

Before long we discovered the marvels of wine in the early evening. Sitting in sidewalk cafes, sipping our Beaujolais, we'd talk about film and gallery openings, dance recitals and Keith Jarrett's latest improvisations at the Arlington. We eventually discovered the California Cabernets that lent themselves so well to the heartier meals we still couldn't quite afford—starving artists that we were. But, as luck would have it, the weather was so incredible we didn't need much food to sustain us through the winter so to speak. We made do with salads, fresh baked breads, good cheeses and an impressive variety of wines.

After a year or two of our polite café society, the nights got a little longer, the drinks got a little stronger and the first clarion call of ambition began revealing ferocious appetites. The music got louder.

The outfits became more sleek and intimidating than sensual and liberating. The banter was all about acquisition and supercharged with style over substance except for those substances used to amuse and abuse. The coupling felt carnivorous as if the players were let out of cages. We buried our tender philosophies, descending to hell in stages.

I had the wonderful good fortune to be reborn not out of any religious awakening, but through a twist of fate that led me to work with children. I was blessed to be able to revisit life through their eyes and in so doing, find a better purpose for a life that was still my own.

I guess life is like a delicate sandwich sometimes. You need to enjoy it before it gets too messy. And if by chance it gets too messy anyway—you will need to clean it up.

Made In Bangalore?

New socks and underwear, now that's the way to start a day! If a decent pair of socks cost about four or five bucks and a good pair of underwear goes for about the same then I should be able to luxuriate for under four grand a year. Of course I know that would be an unthinkable waste not to mention the burden on our local landfill if I managed to start a movement of likeminded connoisseurs of the unmentionable kind. Imagine what future anthropologists would think of us with that kind of find.

These people threw away their undergarments after a single use! Who the hell did they think they were? Midas? We're not talking disposable diapers, but cotton blends in briefs and boxers plus wool acrylic woven footsies to cover all their spoiled little tootsies! In a scant few thousand years, these creatures came from a period of time where a tunic covered everything and was worn until it fell apart to a time when they threw away their own jewel cases rather than wash and reuse them. Oh the insanity—frivolous beasts they must have been!

Given the current economic status, there is very little chance I can convince anyone else to pursue this romantic gesture with me. I'm not even sure I can afford it myself, no matter how tempting it is. I don't drive a fancy car. I don't drink in an upscale bar. I don't live for designer labels nor dine very often at Top Chef Tables. What's so wrong with taking a stance, by starting each day in new underpants? Can't we break out of this proletariat's box, by beginning each day in a fresh pair of sox?

If you've opened a newspaper or gone online, watched television or listened to a radio lately then you know it's impossible to avoid two types of information. One is that we are enduring a bad economy and the other insists that most of us our grossly overweight. On the one hand, we've got to tighten our belt and on the other hand we're clearly anything but svelte. Apparently, we're running out of resources because we've already eaten them? The paradox plays out further, when we're repeatedly informed that the only way out of our economic struggle is for the consumer to start spending more. But if we're already consuming way too freaking much, what the hell would we be spending more for?

About the only thing that makes any sense to me lately is a move towards buying what we produce. You can call it National Pride or Shop Local if you like, but it's an idea whose time has come again. For what it's worth, it's the same mentality Gandhi used to end the British rule when he convinced a billion people to harvest their own salt and start weaving their own clothes. I'm still a little concerned, because I know a good farmer who grows my corn; we've got a great baker, butcher and even candlestick maker, but it's hard to find socks and underwear made in America and I'm determined to live a luxurious life.

Spanish Guitar

I'm trying to plan an elegant summer evening in my mind. It beats spending brain cells on the daily grind. There's a Spanish guitar; isn't there always when the word elegant comes to mind. The women are dressed in light summer dresses revealing their tanned lovely limbs. Who cares what the men are wearing as long as they're pouring wine. Make that Sangria, chilled but rich, red and fruity to go with the tapas that each of them had to design.

The napkins are white and I notice a faint lipstick stain on the one that lies across the plate directly in front of me. Was one of the senoritas trying to send me a message or did I sit at the wrong seat again? I hate when that happens, especially if I start feeling the effects of the wine in the evening before the sun has fully departed. Then through my melancholy haze, I gaze upon el Greco's painted sky holding my head like a screaming Munch before the festivities have even truly begun.

Okay, it's time to wash my face and splash a bit of peppery cologne behind my ears in case my fantasy can hear what I've been thinking. The crowd awaiting the trio is filled with warm and lovely faces. It embraces the light from torches lit to ward off the lazy buzzing moscas who sleep happily near the half eaten morsels left behind by dainty ladies dining delicately to beat the heat. They bring a gentle breeze to those of us sitting near them as they sensually fan their faces with black winged weapons employed in a battle of the flamenco versus our very senses.

The guitar starts slowly with a short string of single notes followed by a flourish strummed with barely enough passion to pull the violin into the fray. A lovely young girl seated on the edge of the audience is wearing a skirt so short that her grandmother wouldn't approve; but the man who looks old enough to be her grandfather seated next to her leers his approval gratefully. She closes her eyes to follow the music. His eyes remain open, but the lids are so heavy they hide where he lands his increasingly lingering glances.

While the guitar and the violin intertwine, couples smile at each other tenderly holding hands. As the tempo increases and a cello gives depth to the sound with an entrance fit for the guest of honor, all hands sweat apart and applaud together as breathing becomes labored, breasts begin to glisten with drops of perspiration and the audience turns it's attention to its own changing dynamic.

Would be lovers steal glances while a happy couple dances. They all take their chances, savoring the nectar of this night. The young and old swoon with the wine and the tune and taste the fragrance of a food fit for gods. The bold and bashful move together, filling each other's needs. For once their purposes are not at odds.

Gato Negro

I had stomach problems when I was a kid, so my grandmother tied a string of garlic around my neck. Peeled, ripe cloves of garlic strung up on eighty pound test, unbreakably knotted around the neck of a sixth grader—what level of hell is that, Mr. Dante? If it wasn't for the fact that some poor schmuck vomited down the staircase all over a few fellow students at Mercerville Elementary that afternoon, I think my vampire repellant secret would have been discovered and I would have been the talk of the town.

I ain't superstitious but a black cat just crossed my path. I almost had to sing that line. We are still a relatively young species, we humans, merely half a million years in the making and barely ten thousand years of it have been studied, documented and available for review and discussion. The early years were definitely given to trial and error on a personal scale while these most recent years seem to be devoted to colossal strides and crashes. If the first time a panther passed in front of you, they ate your firstborn you could be forgiven for developing an adversity to seeing them cross your path. But if the meltdown of a nuclear reactor spews enough radiation to leave a fifty mile radius of scorched earth for the next five millennium, wouldn't it make sense to take a little more precaution the next time you build one?

I'm not sure if there are spirits bumping in the night and for once, I'm not talking about strippers and hookers or players and cheaters. I mean ghouls, ghosts, goblins, gremlins, fairies, phantoms and fantasmas of every imaginable ilk, not to mention the undead whisperers walking in between. But since we haven't been able to establish a scientifically proven link to the afterlife, all theories, fears and assorted religious as well as non religious beliefs are worth considering. If you can't prove a negative assumption then you can't disprove a positive premise either. And speaking of ether—isn't that a gas? So we've found a way back to stomach problems after all.

Some stomach problems are due to a lack of intestinal fortitude. No guts, no glory so the story goes. Well I'm going to share one of those superstitious tidbits that saved me plenty of aggravation a few years back. I can't tell you where it came from, but I can personally vouch for its effectiveness. I was working at a job I hated and the worst part about it was the assistant manager between me and the boss. The boss was a decent guy although he did have a rather large ruler up his ass, but I think I could have gotten along with him under other circumstances. The assistant manager was frankly just a sleazeball. We were in retail and he was a shark, a thief, a snide pretender, befriender of no one if they didn't fill his pockets and he obviously rubbed me the wrong way, day after day after day. Well one night, a bewitching accomplice who must remain nameless wrote this asshole's name on the bottom of my shoe as I sat there complaining about him. I laughed and forgot about it, but wouldn't you know it—the next day this guy couldn't do enough to keep out of my way. I'm telling you he was like a scared little kitty and he never bothered me again from that day on.

All Kinds of Barbecue

I like my eggs over easy and that's not easy to say in Spanish, so when I travel south of the border, things tend to get a little scrambled. One of the first phrases I ever learned in Spanish class was that I like spaghetti and meatballs or "albondigas" in that language. That word has stuck with me some thirty plus years and I have never once had occasion to use it, other than to mention that it was one of the first words I ever learned in Spanish. Maybe if I went to Argentina? There are a lot of Italians there and I'm sure some of them eat "albondigas," although "un buen parrillada" is what they are famous for. That's literally translated as "a good grill," but it implies one of the best barbecue experiences you could ever imagine. My mouth is watering at the thought of Argentinean beef, Chilean wine, Peruvian seafood and a Brazilian woman serving it to me—but I'm sure I've gotten off track if I was ever on one.

Years ago, I spent a few months in a rat infested shack on a beach in Costa Rica finishing my first novel. I swam first thing every morning, bought fruit and fresh baked bread from the locals to go with my cup of tea and then sat on a balcony overlooking the ocean and wrote all day, every day. At night, I drank enough of the local rum and assorted spirits to tolerate the scurrying in the rafters above me. I passed out pretty early and woke up to repeat my self imposed routine.

On Saturday afternoons, I would hike about three or four miles south along a dirt road to the closest little town populated with Euro-hippies, surfers, Rastafarians and a few indigenous family farmers. Tourists also drove a few hours in from the city to spend their weekends at this rustic little port. The atmosphere was like a carnival with food, music, drink and dance and I always stayed a little too long considering the walk back along an unlit path that I usually took alone.

On one of those late Saturday nights, as I staggered back to my shack along the beach, I noticed the blue glow of an old television set coming from my neighbor Fernando's place. There in his little hovel along with the chickens pecking for whatever was left on the dirt floor, sat my neighbor and three of his friends hunkered down around a thirteen inch black and white screen hooked up to a car battery, watching an episode of Dynasty. I don't know how I got so close without them hearing me, but I managed to eavesdrop on their conversation long enough to hear them wonder what the hell I was doing in their neighborhood when clearly everybody in the states lived like the people they were watching on television. I startled them by laughing out loud, but they welcomed me when they saw the half full bottle I was carrying. I don't remember much of the conversation, but I'm absolutely positive they still think I'm nuts to this day. I threw a barbecue—American style with hot dogs and homemade potato salad, beer and sodas for them and their kids before I left. It was the least I could do for their hospitality. I wonder if they would have preferred "albondigas?"

DNA

There but fore a strand or two, I could have been a Nobel laureate, a mass murderer, or even a rhesus monkey. We have so much more in common than the meager threads that separate us from the plant and animal kingdoms let alone our fellow man. History is devoted to the wars we've fought over our differences and Herstory is yet to be told.

I had some wonderful conversations this past weekend with other like minded and equally grateful members of my species. The only real question of any consequence in all of our discussions was "why us?" In our case, I hasten to add, it was never a poor, poor pitiful me lament, but more of a "how did we get so lucky" kind of question. There but fore the Grace of God or a few strands of genetic material, our lives could have been so drastically different. We could be struggling in abject poverty or living opulent lives in fear and misery.

Many of my friends are certain there are no accidents or coincidences and that our lives are filled with meaningful events in order to help us to serve a significant purpose. I like to think I'm here to serve a greater good, but what if my entire raison de etre was simply to pass a kind word onto someone I met in third grade to stop them from becoming Jack the Ripper? Anything else I accomplish would be superfluous and the measure of my existence would be a simple exercise of ego.

In terms of size, our earth is less than a speck of dust compared to the size of our own galaxy let alone the universe. In terms of time, the entire extent of man's existence on this planet is less than the blink of any eye when compared to the light years it takes for light to reach us from distant stars no longer in existence. Isn't it amazing how important we still think we are?

We've built libraries, pyramids, citadels and cathedrals. We've changed the course of rivers to suit our travel plans. We've torn down mountaintops that got in our way. We've sent expeditions to the furthest reaches of our lands and seas and yet none of us can answer that simple question: "why us?"

Even if the religious predictions are right and we survive an Armageddon to thrive a thousand years in peace—what is a thousand years compared to the vast expanse of time that stretches out behind us and before us? Even if we learn to live together in peace and harmony on this tiny speck of dust floating in an ever expanding galaxy in this ever expanding universe, how do we know that some other civilization from someplace far away isn't ready to bowl us over in favor of a quicker route to somewhere we've never even imagined?

As the dolphins sing towards the end of Buckaroo Banzai—"so long and thanks for all the fish." There but fore a couple strands of DNA or the will to understand each other, we could have let them lead the way.

Backstage

Some of my fondest high school memories took place in the auditorium working on one production or another. It gave me a real sense of community. I felt like I belonged there. It was kind of like "Glee" except that no one was openly gay back then and there were no allowances made for any wheelchair bound performers either.

Dealing with homosexuality was tough in those days; especially for those of us that felt at home in the theater. On the one hand, none of us really cared if a guy preferred guys, as long as he didn't ask you to be his doll. On the other hand, I liked sports too and sometimes you had to choose between the two because of scheduling conflicts. I feel bad about those who stayed in the closet, unaware that they could have been open with me. I didn't go out of my way to put them at ease, but I don't think I ever offended them either. I only became aware in adulthood, how an offhand comment from someone you care about can sting for an awfully long time. I hope I didn't wound anyone thoughtlessly by being a macho young man.

As for the fair and opposite sex, I fell in love every other day back then. There was a young nun in the Sound of Music that I was dying to make a habit. The girls that did set design for Gypsy and the Unsinkable Molly Brown stole my heart with every brush stroke they applied. The chorus girls in the South Pacific, the munchkins in the Wizard of Oz, the scantily clad dancers in their dressing rooms reminded me of a Bob Fosse show . . . well you see how I let my imagination carry me away.

And then there were the leading ladies. Sirens, singers and ingénues with presence and ethereal charms—we longed to have them on our arms at cast parties where the paparazzi (or yearbook committee photographer) would catch us laughing deliciously about something so chic and private that only the illuminati was privileged enough to know. It was years before I realized how few of them would ever find themselves upon a stage like that again.

Some of us were grateful for a chance to perform. There were others just as pleased to participate in their own way. It takes a whole lot of people to put on a show. Actors, dancers, set designers, choreographers, singers, musicians, lighting people, sound technicians, graphic artists, ushers, ticket takers, costume designers, seamstresses, props people, show runners, caterers, directors and stage managers not to mention the computer guys on special effects. Of course we didn't have computers back then . . . the orchestra handled the sound effects and created suspense. The lighting people set the mood for whatever storm was supposed to be brewing.

It was magic, pure and simple, like theater is supposed to be and it did all of us a world of good. It might be fun to do it all over again and some of us probably should.

The Sounds of Silence

Have you ever had one of those awkward conversations where you can't seem to get on the same page no matter how hard you try? I'm not talking about trying to communicate with a stranger. I'm talking about a communication breakdown with one of your closest and most trusted friends. You know their heart is in the right place. You know they only have your best interest in mind. You appreciate their keen understanding of the subject matter and yet you can't seem to spit out whatever the hell you're trying to say.

Blah, blah, blah . . . Sometimes we act as if our world revolves around the trials and tribulations of our own bruised egos and forget that the self serving images we mistakenly consider sacrosanct are harmless at best and no match for the breezes that rustle the emerald leaves outside our frame of reference.

This summer, I want to sit out on my back deck with an Absolut and tonic, watch the wind in the trees and listen to some eclectic music. If we have to talk about anything, let's talk about Cezanne's brush strokes. Let's talk about primitive man's need to draw on the walls of his cave. Let's talk about a slice of ripe jersey tomato covered with a thin slice of fresh mozzarella, drizzled with a bit of balsamic glaze and topped with a fresh basil leaf. Let's talk about how freaking lucky we are to live the lives we have.

I'm not taking a long vacation this year, boo hoo! There are people all over the world suffering devastating losses due to economic and environmental disasters. I'm so sick of hearing myself and others just as fortunate complain about anything at all. Frankly, I'm sick of the sound of my own voice and as a writer that's a little tough to put on the page.

Thanks to my daily Zen Calendar, I can share with you what Aldous Huxley once said, "Our goal is to discover that we have always been where we ought to be." I knew a man who knew Huxley years ago and thinking of him is worth my time.

Hallock Hoffman was a robust white haired sixty something Psychologist who flew his own glider plane and founded an educational institute in Santa Barbara, California many years ago. I was in awe of him and never really knew how to speak in his presence. I know that's hard for some of you to believe but it's true. Anyway, one night I dreamed I was sitting in a circle on a cliff overlooking the Pacific and Hallock was standing in the middle trying desperately to communicate something to all of us nonverbally. Whatever it was, I got it. I stood up and walked to him and we hugged each other like long lost friends.

A few days later, I saw him in his office. He stood up and gave me the exact same look. Sometimes I miss those conversations.

Femme Phrenale

Her eyelashes, though exceedingly dark, long and lustrous, could not shield even a casual observer from the otherworldly and compelling quality of her serene cerulean eyes. Her face was framed by short cut bangs that fell gently from auburn highlighted spikes, as if Audrey Hepburn had finally gotten an update without sacrificing any of her classic beauty. The long firm, tanned and toned limbs revealed by a daring slit in her classic black evening gown were both sensual and athletic, enough to leave a man light-headed from a lingering glance. Her story and the fantasies she inspired would only grow more alluring as the night went on.

She moved catlike to a corner table and established a view of the entire room, but was it meant to see or be seen? She ordered a dirty martini in a voice the cocktail waitress later said was infused with a slight and sexy rasp, deeper than her slender young frame would have led one to anticipate. She held a long thin white cigarette to her slightly pursed lips and it was lit by a self assured potential suitor who had gauged his approach to full advantage and took the time while proffering a match to notice that she wore no telltale engagement or wedding ring. Her smile was pleasant but perfunctory and however she responded to his usually successful overture was direct and to the point, sending him straight back to a barstool in a cold sweat unable to explain what had just happened.

In short order, two more able bodied lotharios would be similarly dispensed with before the mysterious attraction signaled the waitress for attention. She rejected a third pretender's offer of a drink and ordered a good bottle of Chardonnay with a single glass insisting that she would be settling her own accounts this evening. After approving the wine, she requested a tuna tartar, a chilled gazpacho and a dozen raw oysters.

Nearly everyone in the restaurant felt as if she ate her meal in slow motion. They savored every bite she took and felt a surge of excitement as the shellfish slid down her throat inside that lovely long and graceful neck. She glowed more beautifully with her second and third glass of wine and by the time she wiped her mouth with the corner of a linen napkin, the owner knew he could have sold it as a souvenir.

She stretched languorously and signaled her server who rushed to be near her and stood there tongue tied. She ordered a dark chocolate truffle and two snifters of the house's finest brandy and went to the restroom to freshen up. When she returned, a disheveled looking man in a herringbone tweed coat and button down shirt had taken the other seat at her table without anyone even noticing his arrival. The other patrons looked on in awe as she leaned across the table and kissed him full and long. She couldn't keep her hands off of him while he sipped his warm libation and regaled her with statistics from his latest trials, eager to share the results of his lifelong research.

When the check came, he sheepishly allowed her to pay, muttering something about how embarrassing it was to be a kept man. The Femme Phrenale paid no attention to the dumbstruck onlookers as she took her Nobel prizewinner by the arm and led him home.

BYOB

There's always somebody ahead of the curve. I had a friend who died a few years back and it has taken me a long time to appreciate how advanced some of his ideas were. I can't reveal them all because I'm still hoping to cash in on one or two of them, but he did predict the e-Reader, as well as the rise of social networking.

When it comes to real estate or more specifically exotic beachfront locales, you have to follow the hippies. They get there first looking for the next unspoiled spot on the planet to meditate and vegetate upon. They are quickly followed by the surfers seeking an ultimate wave to ride. The tourists show up as soon as there are puka shell necklaces and tie dyed tee shirts for sale alongside a hip vegetarian pizza joint that stocks plenty of cold beer. Before this reaches the point of popularity the developers show up to buy off the locals landlords and the dance of the dollar sign begins. On a positive note, the roads get paved and everything else gets a facelift. The sanitation upgrades are a boon to the local labor force and construction feeds the families that are driven out of their homes because they can no longer afford the rental rates on such newly desirable addresses. Friends told me this is what happened in Indonesia. I saw it happen in Costa Rica and Belize, but I may be able to beat them to the next undiscovered gem. I'm not telling anyone where it is until I open my Bed & Bottleshop.

If you're considering when to invest in a particular city neighborhood, then you have to scout out the gay community. Nothing can wipe out urban blight, like good looking people who can boogie all night. I'm not being flip or facetious. I'm serious when it comes to food and fashion. Galleries, nightclubs, trendy shops, restaurants, spas and chic salons can turn around metro decay faster than you can spell sashay. If you're not secure enough in your hetero, then this is no place for you to go. Consider investing in something rural. I hear the Balkans are nice.

Technology rewards the nerd for years of sacrifice. It may not be easy for them to find mates but they're beginning to create their own companions. They could live longer and healthier lives than their intellectually challenged backers but they will definitely need to protect themselves from well funded unscrupulous hackers. I may want my general practitioner to have a holistic approach, but if and when I need a surgeon, I'm looking for one with a laser sharp focus. I'm cool with a wide range of ancient healing arts, but if my malady is diagnosed as aggressive and modern, then let's skip the hocus pocus.

There's cutting edge and bleeding edge and it's up to us to know the difference. Some say, you shouldn't risk more than you can afford to lose. Others say go big or go home. Trendsetters are necessarily risk takers. They just see things a little differently. They view life itself as an adventure and they enjoy the journey. There goal is not to do more, be more or have more. There goal is just to see more. They get there before the rest of us, because they're willing to let go of what they've already enjoyed. I've got me a few ideas and I've stolen a few along the way. I'm going open a place to party for the married, straight singles, couples and gay. It's going to be on a beachfront that very few have seen. I'll promote it on Facebook, but you'll have to buy MYbook to find it. I'm going to hire the locals to run it based on a nerd's design. I'm going to serve you fresh local foods and insist that you share your wine.

SongMaker

Sometimes you have to let go. Plant yourself in the moment and make the most of whatever comes your way. Everything can change in an instant and the things that you hold dear can disappear. Life as we know it includes the certainty of suffering and even the innocent pay a price for this existence.

There are wise men and women wandering the planet; speaking at symposiums, holding prayer vigils and meditating on honor and balance. They serve as counterpoint to despots, murderers and thieves who would sell their soul for quick profit in defiance of the long term consequences.

There are humble servants of good and true ideals who live unassuming lives and eat modest meals. They have chosen a path instead of a lifestyle. They are too kind to laugh at those of us who cling to our comforts and hide behind our possessions. They seek nothing in this life and welcome the emptiness. Their efforts enable them to glimpse self-fulfillment. Our holdings alone can keep us from such revelations.

Once I walked away from the things of this world and rode upon the four winds. I heard the mountain's song and knew the ocean's symphony. The green grass waved a welcoming my way and birds greeted me as one of their own. The air was sweet with nectar and the gods accepted my gifts. I embraced the ten thousand things and we were one. There was nothing left for me but to return.

I'm a man of this world which is of my own making and I need to take responsibility for the actions I am taking. If I am kind let it bring kindness. If I am cold, let it bring cold. When I am willing to share, let it be something bold. When I'm ready to learn, let the teacher appear. When it's time for me to teach, let it not be out of fear.

I walked out of the Andes Mountains nearly a quarter of a century ago after earning the right to be what I had already become—a SongMaker. I came roaring down from the heights on wings of laughter and have been laughing at myself fairly often ever after. With a right to write and a will to live, I became a person with something to give and I found someone who accepted my gift.

I came back into the modern world slowly, circuitously building a better foundation. My wife and I were blessed beyond belief with a child born of our better selves. We've formed friendships worthy of being called treasures and established business and community relationships enough to provide for our needs. Now as we get older, the time is coming to harvest our seeds. If we planted love and laughter, let it rain back down on all around us freely. Let it grow to soften the blow of any near us who would suffer this life sadly. If we took good care of our garden, let it care for us in return. If we planted art and nature, let them continue to guide us home again and again.

Home is where the art is . . .

I grew up in a decidedly white working class neighborhood called Mercerville. My high school graduating class of several hundred students only had about ten or fifteen black kids and fewer Hispanics than that. Seven miles away in downtown Trenton, New Jersey they had the reverse of what we had. I was a sophomore in 1968 when the riots started. I'll never forget the look on Nate Palmer's face when he told me in no uncertain terms to stay the hell out of downtown Trenton that day. Nate and I played basketball together and if memory serves me well, we also sang together in the choir. We considered each other friends although we'd never been in each other's home nor even met each other's parents.

Julio was a different story. He transferred into our school system from Kingston, north of Princeton where there had been a larger Latino population. He was an extremely intelligent and likeable person who was able to blend easily into our lily white world, dating popular girls, playing sports, excelling in classes and even becoming our class president. Sadly, most of the people in our school at that time would have been surprised to find out that his parents spoke Spanish at home. For me it was a chance to finally practice what I was studying and we were more than welcome in each other's homes.

I left New Jersey in my late teens, bound for sunny southern California for a variety of reasons. One was adventure—I was sure I had the makings of a rock star in me. Another was sheer boredom for where I was—Rider University, a noted business college at the time didn't inspire me any more than my working class neighborhood. The only exciting things in my life back then were my regular visits to Princeton, a mere ten miles away but representing an entirely different view of the world, and my frequent jaunts into New York City. I was convinced that the world was a vast and wonderful place to explore and that my narrow minded neighborhood was not very representative of the life I wanted to live.

For the next eighteen years I made a living at odd jobs but mainly pursued a career of sorts in music and entertainment. I lived in Santa Barbara, California for about eight or nine years, working there and in Los Angeles. I traveled all over North and South America playing with stellar musicians, writing the great American novel and meeting incredible people. I met and married my second wife in Lima, Peru. We managed a horseback riding resort in Belize and then went to live in Miami Beach, Florida. The thought that I would ever come back to live in New Jersey could not have been further from my mind. All of that changed when my daughter was born.

I was working for a Spanish Language publisher at the time and they asked me to help expand their New York business. We went to visit family in New Jersey and my wife fell in love with the place. I'm not sure how much Mercerville has changed, but Lawrenceville is where we live now. It is a hodgepodge of every race, religion and social situation known to man and we love it. We are ten miles away from the cultural and educational events in Princeton; an hour's train ride to Manhattan; a forty-five minute drive to Philadelphia; an hour from the shore. It's a great place to raise a kid and a better place to live than I had ever imagined when I was one. I'm not sure which of us has grown up—me or New Jersey and I surely hope my traveling days are far from over, but it's nice to see that some things do change over the years.

Abundant Lives

In the next twelve months, someone you know will give birth and someone you know will die. They probably won't have any connection, but the cycle of our lives plays to a balance nonetheless. It's hard to deny the rhythm of life, when you live where there are four distinct seasons. Here in the northeast the trees are bare and there's frost on our windshields some mornings. A hot cup of tea makes you gaze out the window watching birds fly south and wishing you could join them. You hunker down by a fireplace, hoping you chopped enough wood. Then loving the smell and the crackle, you realize life is good.

I've never been a fan of the winter, but something inside me is changing. I'm more anxious to shed my attachment to what I want than I am to shed my clothes and lie in the sun. What I want doesn't matter and it never did. It will always miss the point. We're here to enjoy what is, not what's missing. If the present has passed before we've borne witness, then we might as well let it go. If the future is ours to shape then the past holds what we need to know.

One riddle in life is why it takes so long for a singer to truly understand his own song. You can capture a melody and pause for effect, but the grace notes are graceless if you don't connect. Your heart and mind must surrender and fall in order to know that you've given your all. In the moment it takes for a soul to awake, the earth itself will quiver and shake. Nothing can stand in the way of true beauty and honoring that is an artist's duty.

As another year ends, it's time to ponder just what wonders lie out yonder. We are filled with a gentleness many years old to ward off the biting nature of cold. Loved ones lost are found in memories rekindled and the strength of our hearts remains undwindled. We smile at the sight of a newborn child, touched by a light so tender and mild. We relight the candles of hope and concern assured that the light of love will still burn.

In the next few days we have time to prepare for a year ahead in which we deeply care. Let us give our hearts to a loving embrace and allow ourselves a state of grace. We all know so deeply in our very being, the things that bind and the things that are freeing. So if we must be bound to anything, let us bind ourselves to the joy that life brings. Let us give thanks for abundant lives and be willing to share in each other's sorrow. We can only live life day by day, and dream of a bright tomorrow.

Author Biography

John Calu has worked in Entertainment, Education and Corporate America. His writing combines the lessons he's learned in each of those endeavors and he appreciates the opportunity to share his insights with a growing audience.